HOW TO STAY
and not flee

STORIES FROM ONE
MISSIONARY FAMILY'S
FIRST DECADE OVERSEAS

VERONICA STONE

Publisher's Note: This is a narrative nonfiction memoir. The events and conversations contained in this book have been documented to the best of the author's ability. Some names and identifying details have been changed to protect the privacy of individuals.

Scripture quotations marked CSB have been taken from the Christian Standard Bible®, Copyright © 2017 by Holman Bible Publishers. Used by permission. Christian Standard Bible® and CSB® are federally registered trademarks of Holman Bible Publishers.

Scripture quotations marked (NIV) are taken from the Holy Bible, New International Version®, NIV®. Copyright © 1973, 1978, 1984, 2011 by Biblica, Inc.™ Used by permission of Zondervan. All rights reserved worldwide. www.zondervan.com The "NIV" and "New International Version" are trademarks registered in the United States Patent and Trademark Office by Biblica, Inc.™

Scripture quotations marked (NLT) are taken from the Holy Bible, New Living Translation, copyright ©1996, 2004, 2015 by Tyndale House Foundation. Used by permission of Tyndale House Publishers, Carol Stream, Illinois 60188. All rights reserved.

Cover design and image by Veronica Stone
Edited by Danelle Young, DanelleYoung.com
Proofread by Eunice Hahn
Book Layout © 2017 BookDesignTemplates.com

To Stay or Flee / Veronica Stone -- 1st ed.
ISBN 979-8-9886924-0-9 (paperback)
ISBN 979-8-9886924-1-6 (e-book)
Library of Congress Control Number: 2023912763

Dedicated to my adventuresome crew who have my back on the field and in the battle.

Abe and Anna,

I hope these stories bring smiles to your faces. I'm grateful every day for your willingness to follow the call with us. Although you didn't choose to live this life between continents, you embrace it with joy and perseverance. I pray you will learn the most important lesson—God alone is our refuge. In Him, we find peace.

Ron,

At seventeen, I never imagined you were the man I'd marry. I certainly didn't imagine this would be our life together. I'm so thankful the Lord, in His grace, knew I would need someone as calm and cool as you to face life's challenges. Thank you for encouraging me to process our hard places through words.

Foreword

Several years ago, on a cool fall day, I sat eating tomato soup in a friend's cozy Midwest kitchen. She shared a piece of advice over that meal I will never forget. Already well into her retirement years, Charmaine had weathered the ebbs and flows of life. She and her husband kept their hands to the plow for years, serving the Lord. He had moved them from place to place. Each time, they surrendered to the Lord and followed His lead. They had experienced their fair share of sorrow and trials.

As I lamented about a painful situation, I admitted I was afraid. I didn't know how to trust God through a trial this big. I can still hear Charmaine's voice as she interjected, "Now honey, you know how to get through this. You can trust God through this too. You just look back! When we look back and see what God has brought us through, it gives us the faith to move forward and trust Him in the next storm."

This book was written in large part due to this advice. In 2022, we were in the most violent battle we had ever been through, spiritually speaking. I knew God wanted us to move forward in our ministry, but I was frozen in fear. What would happen to my kids? My marriage? Our families and friends expressed concern. So I looked back. I began writing about the past decade we'd spent overseas—funny moments, outrageous ordeals, and hard times. I had two objectives. First, I needed to be reminded of all God had brought us through to find the faith to move forward. It was an intense season. Second, I desperately wanted to compile stories from our life overseas for our kids while I could remember them.

I did not initially intend to write a book. I started by sitting in front of my computer, focused on recalling and recording God's faithfulness in the past. Somehow, as I wrote, a theme emerged—how to stay and not flee. It was as if the Lord was taking my hand and walking me through each instance when I failed to fully trust Him. He reminded me of His faithfulness again and again as I typed each story, sometimes laughing, sometimes crying.

Writing this book has been the very thing that's kept me from fleeing during this challenging season. Please know my goal as a missionary isn't to stay physically somewhere, but in the center of His will, staying engaged at a location until the cloud of the Lord moves us onward. I hope this book will help you think back through your own story and step forward in faith. Because as Charmaine said, "You can trust God through this too. You just look back! When we look back and see what God has brought us through, it gives us the faith to move forward and trust Him in the next storm."

Contents

CHAPTER 1

Hard Goodbyes

When the Lord Prepared Us to Go

Dungy

I climbed the basement staircase with tears in my eyes. This was it. We had surrendered to the call, sold our home, and quit our jobs. We were moving overseas, and now we faced the most painful part of the process. Looking into the face of my brown-eyed girl before bed, my eyes welled up with tears. How could I leave this sweet pup to travel to the other side of the planet? Was it really God's will for me? Would she remember me if I ever saw her again? Would she even be alive?

After climbing the stairs, I slumped onto the sofa with an obvious sigh that said I needed to talk. My mom looked over, noticed the tears, and offered a compassionate look. My twenty-six-year-old self morphed into an emotional mess. This was the hardest goodbye yet, because this time, it wasn't just for a year. This move would be long-term. Life in America wouldn't be the same when we returned.

But the nagging ache in my heart that night wasn't from how America would change while we lived abroad. It wasn't from leaving my parents, my sister, or even Chick-fil-A (although I would miss them all terribly). It was from the soft brown eyes of a pooch who had walked with me through countless hard days. What would happen to this brilliant golden retriever? She was more like a child than a pet and would soon be homeless. How many times had she walked into school by my side and helped put struggling students at ease? Her patient disposition and unwillingness to leave an outcast alone preached to me as much as my dad's Sunday sermons did.

And now what was the plan? We had none. We couldn't expect her to be transported from here to there during our language study or to physically adapt to life on the equator. It was unreasonable to bring her along. My parents preferred not to have an indoor dog. The rest of our family was far away. Oh, how my heart ached thinking about giving her to a random person we may or may not see again. As a waterfall of tears streamed down my face, I squeaked out to my mom, "But Dungy." Then she said the magic words: "Okay honey, we'll keep her." Immediately, my anxiety eased.

Goodbyes were rough, but some felt unbearable while we prepared to move halfway around the world. They would pop up and unexpectedly overtake my entire being. Some people struggle to say goodbye to a special possession that can't come along, a relative whose health is uncertain, or a special happy place they will miss. For me, it was my dog. For some reason, I mourned leaving that brown-eyed pooch more than I mourned all the other goodbyes.

Decisions

Preparing to move to another country evoked a range of emotions within me. One day, it would thrill me to learn exciting details about our new city, house, or my job. The next day, I'd be in tears because I realized it was the last time I would do something like go to the post office. My rollercoaster of emotions soared to the sky and then crashed to the ground, all while I made major decisions about what to keep, what to store, and what to take.

Decisions had to be made about how to schedule our last weeks, what to give to our family to say goodbye well, and what to take with us to help with the inevitable homesickness. Demands for decisions pummeled me like the wind and rain of a relentless hurricane, challenging me continuously to respond. My emotions yanked and pulled me in all directions until I could hardly decide on anything, let alone set up my new home in a foreign country.

Through all the waves of emotion during our preparation period, I hadn't even considered the question that would be the refrain of our life overseas: Once we get to this foreign land, how will we stay and not flee out of fear?

Our First Set of Goodbyes
When the Lord first gave us the idea to work overseas, it wasn't through a calling to be missionaries. It was an opportunity to work abroad and do something new. Our first set of goodbyes was difficult, but there were few strings attached. It was our first time on a long-haul flight. Our hearts felt the gravity of the miles that would be between us and the United States, but we planned to return home eleven months later. Our brown-eyed girl was only one at the time and would be a healthy two-year-old when we got back. Our parents were still young and active. We weren't liquidating our American life.

However, over the course of that first year in a foreign country, we realized the Lord wanted us to live overseas long-term and for a spiritual purpose. A few years later, we said our goodbyes again, this time more permanently. God tends to work that way, doesn't He? We're given little pieces of our puzzle without knowing God's end game. If we could see the big picture at the beginning, we'd probably mess it up.

That first goodbye was more exciting than it was tough. We had a party with our small group and played *Rock Band* until the middle of the night. We reasoned that since we were moving to a time zone exactly twelve hours apart from ours, it only made sense to stay up until the middle of the night to change our body clocks. We acted like we were sixteen again, chugging all the Dr Pepper and Barq's Root Beer we could before our feet arrived at the door of the plane the next morning. Yet, even amid the joy of that party while indulging in the last of our American junk food, I had a moment when it hit. This was our last night in America. My stomach collapsed as I sat on the couch watching my friends sing. This was it. Was this supposed to be it forever? I had a feeling my life would never be the same.

The reasons behind our two moves were vastly different. Those reasons were (and still are) part of the answer to the question: How do we stay and not flee? When we first traversed the Atlantic Ocean, we were fresh out of college on the hunt for adventure. Although God sparked the idea and opened the door, we saw it as a chance to experience a different culture—an exploration. It was not about anything overly spiritual.

Leap of Faith

Adventure called, but the process of making it to the airplane wasn't easy for me. I have a very weird, conflicting personality. While in college, I was so far on the type A scale that I practically broke it. During student teaching, the teacher's aide in my classroom enjoyed purposely moving the pencils and notebooks on my desk just an inch, knowing I would notice and move them back. As passionate (a.k.a. controlling) as I am about structure and order, I'm equally passionate about exploring anything new. I hate monotony. These two characteristics are contradictory and should not coexist in a human body. In the spirit of gaining new life experiences, the trailblazer in me tends to jump off cliffs and commit to wild ideas before I fully think through the implications. Shortly into the free fall, panic spreads through my body as I realize I do not have control of the situation I've just initiated. I imagine when God created me, His thought process was, "Okay, we're going to make this one very orderly. She'll marry someone who is the opposite. They'll drive each other nuts, but that will file off their rough edges. I've given her some structure, but I'm debating her tolerance for adventure. She's going to be a strong one!

Oh, Michael, you did what? You dropped an entire container of adventure in her? I just put an entire container of order in her! *Yikes!* Well, she's going to be fun to watch."

My decision to move to another country demonstrated the wacky way my brain works. I was casually filling out an online application to accept a teaching position offered to me. I had already verbally accepted. This position was ideal, the one I imagined obtaining after college. Then in a *"Squirrel!"* type moment, I noticed an advertisement to teach English in South Korea. I texted my husband Ron, "Haha! There's an ad for teaching in Korea. That would be fun." A week later, I turned down my dream teaching contract to pursue who-knows-what-in-who-knows-where. Great idea, right? My adventurous heart pulled me toward Korea on a whim. Ron happily joined the ride in his laid-back, always-game style. The day of the final decision, we ate bibimbap at a Korean restaurant in our town and dreamed about all the adventure to come. Then about a week later, as I turned in my official rejection letter for my dream teaching contract, panic mode activated. Questions flooded my mind, each more hysterical than the previous. How do you even sit on a plane for 10 hours? What if we don't like the food? How do you grocery shop without a car? Will people understand us? Was this school real? Would we get there and have real jobs, or would this be some phantom school that they said was a school but wasn't really a school? Is there a chance they were actually going to kidnap us and demand a ransom from my family? What if they poisoned us with kimchi so they could steal all our belongings? Maybe we were about to be part of the story-line of *Taken 3* without even knowing it. My skydive toward "Let's do something crazy!" turned into a nosedive toward disaster as I imagined the wildly improbable consequences of my decision on a whim.

Packing

Before you assume I'm a nutcase, that was back in the day before all questions were fully Googleable. The contact person for our questions was not responsive, so I feel a portion of my panic was reasonable. I went into overdrive to compensate for my adventurous I-didn't-think-this-through decision. We purchased every travel guide for South Korea we could find to read up on the culture, landscape, money, and anything else that seemed important to know. Looking back, spiraling out of control after making this decision was comical. Pride kept me from backing out. Instead, I put all my energy into being sure we had every item we could possibly need during our eleven months overseas. We packed more suitcases than I'd like to admit—yes, ten bags for two people. But they only contained the necessities, according to spiraling control freak Veronica:

- Eleven sticks of powder-fresh deodorant
- Two bottles of shampoo per person
- Two bottles of soap per person
- Two containers of Cavender's Greek Seasoning
- A set of queen sheets
- A comforter
- Six boxes of macaroni and cheese
- Four bath towels
- Dry-erase markers
- Notebooks
- Classroom posters
- Puzzles
- Workbooks for teaching
- Beef jerky and assorted snacks

I attribute overpacking to an impulsive decision made by a control freak who was trying to tell herself it would be okay. Ron was annoyingly calm and cool the whole time, even about my excessive purchases (that I deemed necessities) for our move abroad. Though I proposed the idea of moving to a country far away to do who knows what, Ron encouraged me to pursue the idea. I marveled at how God gave him a sense of adventure with next to no angst. I guess God, in His grace, knew I would freak out enough for the two of us.

In the months leading up to our move, I emailed and called our new boss often, requesting clarification on what our "furnished house" in Seoul contained. Now obsessing over my not-well-thought-out choice, I told myself if I just asked enough questions, I would feel confident our soon-to-be boss wasn't a serial killer. However, the responses I received were more like grunts than actual answers . . . though I'm not sure how that's even possible via email.

Sidebar: An Explanation of Asian Grunts
By the way, have you ever analyzed the grunts where you live? I've gotten so fluent in Asian *ehs* that I now know how to translate them into full sentences. This is key to effective language learning. These grunts will guide you into a deeper understanding of your incompetence—or competence if you're lucky. There's the "eh?" with a questioning tone. If you've asked a question and got this eh, you were misunderstood but should try again. However, if it was from a friend, they are likely saying, "Really? I can't believe that." There's also the "eh eh." This one is a quick repeated sound that means, "Yes, that's right." But if someone has no clue what you're saying or asking, they may use this eh just to get you to go away. Translating this grunt properly requires seeing someone's face. If their eyes are bright, then congratulations! You got a

solid yes. If their eyes look as if they aren't registering, they are kindly asking you to stop talking so you can stop embarrassing yourself. Next, there's the solid tone "eh." That means, "I noticed you said something to me, but I either don't understand, don't know the answer, or don't care." That grunt tells you to stop asking questions or find someone else to ask your question to. Then there is the "ehhhhhhh!" drawn out with inflection. This eh translates as, "Yes! How have you taken so long to figure this out?! Wow! You are more incompetent than I previously estimated." Although this is the direct translation, as a traveler in a foreign land, this eh is the one you want to hear, and it's a source of pride, especially if you get to it quickly.

Amid the holy-cow-what-did-we-just-commit-to panic, the "eh" replies from our boss-to-be sparked more spiraling. Our knowledge of expat life was limited to what we saw on TV. We had no experience to know how to plunge in with grace.

South Korea
Our stay in Korea was short. We camped there for eleven months. Then the Lord moved us to a new place. On the hard days of those eleven months when I missed America, I would ask myself, "Why am I here again?" Pictures of Korean palaces, waterfalls where we swam with

friends, and live missile launchers on the 38th parallel (near the DMZ) all flashed in my head. One wrong turn led to multiple machine guns pointing at us. All these things, in some odd way, were exactly what I had hoped for in our time overseas, but the mix of excitement and fear could be overwhelming at times. I would tell myself, "Veronica, this is the price of adventure. Find a new adventure today and push through the tough stuff." Those adventures are now fun memories we'll share with our kids and grandkids.

The question of "Why am I here?" is precursory to a more important question: "Will I stay, or will I flee?" Sometimes the second question comes to mind because the Lord is truly preparing our hearts for a move, and it's time to pack up camp like the Israelites and follow the cloud of the Lord to a new place. But often, the second question pops up as an afterthought because we were already packing up the tent, Lord's will or not. Answering "Why am I here?" is the foundation for our answer to "Will I stay, or will I flee?" Working out our "why" about serving somewhere is imperative if we want to stay put until the Lord instructs us to pick up our tent and move onward.

Life-Changing Experiences

After eleven months in Seoul, the Lord took us back to the US. But during our last few months in Korea, He sowed seeds of a new calling in our hearts. In the second semester, our school received a new eighth-grade student. Anne was brilliant but shy and not Korean like our other students. As we learned about her background, we found that she had never seen a Bible. Her mom, a government official from a country not receptive to Christianity, moved to Korea for work. Our small Christian school happened to be her pick out of all the schools in Seoul.

Anne was inquisitive and analytical. I treasured opportunities to make crafts together at my house and talk about Scripture. Her questions about morality, Jesus, and the prophets reminded me of my informal theological training that happened on horseback with my dad. I loved digging into Scripture and having someone challenge my understanding and ability to communicate truths from the Word of God.

Just after we left Seoul, Anne messaged me to share that she had chosen to follow Jesus. For the first time in my life, I was able to witness an individual transition from never having seen or heard Scripture to choosing the Lord's path with all their heart. This experience wasn't just life-changing for Anne; it was life-changing for me too. The Lord used her curious questions to spark passion in my heart for people who don't have access to Scripture.

Over spring break, Ron had a similar encounter. He chaperoned a group of our high schoolers on a mission trip to a neighboring country. On this trip, the Youth With A Mission (YWAM) leaders hosting the team mandated that each person share their testimony both in a large group setting and one-on-one on the side of a street. This was completely out of Ron's comfort zone, but the students he was with prodded him to go first each time. A funny thing happened on that trip. Ron was different when he came home. Street evangelism was still intimidating to him, but he had felt the Holy Spirit move. His candor as he spoke about sharing with complete strangers was an obvious arrow pointing to our next step in life.

After these life-changing experiences in Korea, we realized God had us camped there for much more than adventure. Excitement to explore a new land took us to Korea, but we brought back more than souvenirs. A new calling stowed away on our plane and followed us home.

A New Calling

As the Lord worked in our hearts, He dangled another opportunity for adventure to catch our attention. We decided flying straight back to the United States would be a waste considering travel within Asia was so cheap. Somehow, we convinced our soon-to-be ex-boss to buy us tickets back to the US routing through a different country. We would cover the difference in cost and get a new passport stamp along the way. As we initiated this plan for adventure, our transformed hearts wouldn't allow us to vacation without a mission. One thing led to another, ending with us hopping on a plane to a place we had never heard of to spend ten days sharing the gospel alongside two missionaries who worked with unreached people.

During those ten days, we met people in the marketplace and their homes, thanks to the two missionaries who served as translators for our "curious traveler" questions. My heart jumped with joy when I observed this couple sharing the story of Abraham with a family who had never heard God's Word. With Anne still on my mind, this opportunity to share with people—never touched by God's Word and without access to church—caused my heart to skip a beat. Ron and I had changed. Our hearts were different. We realized we had a new calling. It was to be a light to these people in this nation where the story of Jesus had not previously been shared.

After a few years of preparation and seminary in the United States, we traveled back to Asia to live among these unreached people. This time our "Why are we here?" was answered by familiar faces of people who did not know the love of a Savior who forgives freely and deeply. Our new "why" would precipitate a new response to "How do you stay and not flee?"

CHAPTER 2

Stolen Beef Jerky

When Laughter Really Is the Best Medicine

Life overseas brought with it a range of emotions we didn't know were possible. It's like weather in the Midwest. In Indiana, we might see snow and sun on the same day. In life overseas, my best conversation in that language might fall on day three of a water outage that has us washing dishes in the rain. Keeping our expectations in check and living lightheartedly is our game plan for taking on hard days. And for taking on travel days.

A PhD in Long Haul Packing
We left the US on our first overseas journey with ten bags packed to the brim with "necessities." We were heading

to South Korea to teach. However, this was prior to acquiring a PhD in Long Haul Packing. This PhD is time consuming to obtain because a person can only earn it after traversing the globe multiple times. It requires strong analytical skills, planning, and determination. The benefit of this honorary degree is the ability to pack while factoring available time, quantity of stuff, and other logistics.

To obtain this degree, first, a traveler needs to calculate the number of days or weeks they'll need beforehand to pack their suitcases based on the type of trip. For instance, preparing for a domestic trip is a packing job one can easily complete the night before leaving, even for a type A personality like me. Once someone has hopped on a plane a few dozen times, they'll likely know what they need for a basic short-term trip. And since they tend to keep those items on hand, they'll be ready to go within a few hours. However, if an expat is flying back to their host country from their motherland, taking a few months to pack slowly will help them better prepare.

Second, a globetrotter needs to calculate the number and type of belongings they can pack based on the airline's allotted weight limit. This part of the packing PhD program is challenging, especially when preparing to live in a new country for the first time. Family members will gift the children enough toys and candy to fill ten times their allotted suitcase space. Because dependent children need clothes (which are usually cheaper and better quality in the motherland), parents need to purge non-essentials before returning overseas. This purge will be Mom's least favorite responsibility when living life between two continents.

A child will expect every McDonald's Happy Meal toy they've collected during the six months in their passport country to fit in one of their two suitcases. Young children have limited spatial awareness. They cannot compare the size and quantity of their toys to the size and quantity of their suitcases. Sorry to say this, but Mom must inevitably be the bad guy who bears the bad news or finds another way to separate her child from their plastic friends.

A smart solution is gradually "losing" certain toys in the months or weeks leading up to departure. This will lessen the grief and despair a child feels when parting with her favorite Barbie (the one with one arm and a crooked head). A good friend or a keenly aware family member can help with the dirty work.

Broaching this subject with family isn't easy. Parents need to find a gentle, indirect way to say, "Dear family, we are taking a plane home, but it's not *our* plane. We are sharing it with approximately 849 other people who are taking their own luggage. While we love your generosity, our daughter cannot fit a life-sized Barbie in her suitcase along with an adequate amount of underwear." In Grandma's defense, her sweet grandbabies have been gone for three or four years. Three years of birthday and Christmas presents for a six-year-old takes up a lot of space!

Finally, to achieve a PhD in Long Haul Packing, one must know how to pack to make unpacking seamless. This level of packing will make any onlooker gawk and wonder, "How did she do it? We asked her if she had an extra hair tie, and she was like, 'Oh sure, I packed those in the bag with the purple string on it in the bottom left corner. That's where all my extra hair supplies are.'" Once a jet-setter hits this level of expertise, they are a boss and should travel like one. I say, "Fling the already-opened plane doors wide as you disembark and walk into that concourse with confidence. Let your wild I've-been-on-a-plane-for-eighty-three-hours hair fly! Your spandex pants that are clearly not business caszh don't even matter. You have a PhD."

This level of certification in Long Haul Packing is a badge of honor one should be proud of. A person can pack two months ahead, knowing what they will need during transit and the days after landing. Experience teaches us what our jet-lagged selves will want first, and that guides our packing decisions. When a woman is this experienced, her husband might say, "Honey, where is the small screwdriver set I got for Christmas?" And even though she's not sure what continent they're standing on, she'll be able to find that exact item for him in a few short minutes. Travelers deserve a round of applause when they're able to pack this efficiently.

Beef Jerky in Beijing

Our first emotional roller-coaster ride overseas ended with a simple solution: take a picture for proof and laugh about it. This may sound basic, but it's an important skill to acquire when you move to the other side of the world.

When we flew internationally for the first time, we were far from PhDs. We were on the adventure of a lifetime, traveling to South Korea as teachers, and still working on our GED in Long Haul Packing. We had plans to drop eight of our ten bags with our boss in Korea, then jump on a plane the next day to go to the Olympics in China. It was the first time we had worked internationally. And yes, it was also the first time we'd been outside the United States, aside from a cruise ship stop in the Bahamas.

We persuaded our boss to buy us tickets that would land in Seoul early so we could hop over to China for the Olympics before we began teaching. When I get an idea in my head, I'm not great at dropping it. I am very convincing. I like to think of it as a strength, but those around me may feel differently. The problem with this plan was that when I packed our bags in America, I didn't think about our trip to China. Again, at that point, I was only beginning the GED program in Long Haul Packing. Packing cubes and other travel hacks weren't on my radar. I couldn't even fit what I wanted to take into the allotted number of bags. That meant when we arrived in Seoul, we had to unpack and repack ten bags in a matter of an hour or two while our boss (who spoke very little English) watched over our shoulders. I can't imagine what he thought when he saw our bottles of soap, tubes of toothpaste, and boxes of dry erase markers. "Wow, these Americans must think there is no soap outside of the United States." To be honest, I'm surprised we made it to China without forgetting underwear.

After twelve hours in Seoul, while waiting for our brains to make it to Asia (I think they were still hovering somewhere over Hawaii), we traveled back to the airport for a flight to China. Our first international adventure was about to begin! On that first trip, making our way through the airports felt like walking through a mirror maze. So much thought went into where we went next. We were the wide-eyed wanderers reading all the signs. Every few minutes, we made sure we had all our belongings, including our passports. (My grandpa convinced me someone *would* try to snatch our passports.) Finally, we landed in China. It was such a rush! We had two stamps on our passports already! Signs about the Olympics lined the terminals, creating an atmosphere of excitement!

Our now very exhausted bodies waited for our two bags at the carousel. I'd attached a brightly colored ribbon to each for easy spotting. Gold star for me! I read that tip on this somewhat new thing called the internet. It worked like a charm. We quickly identified our bags and retrieved them. Before we left, we snapped a picture with two Olympic mascots in the airport. Ah, the adventure begins!

Standing in the crowded airport hall in front of us was a Chinese policeman. There's a certain fear that strikes when seeing a police officer in a foreign country. This was my first time feeling that fear. Alongside this police officer, though, was something I had never seen: a beagle dog wearing an official police harness, with sad eyes and floppy ears that nearly dragged on the ground. His eyes just screamed, "I need a hug!" What a hilarious sight to see! A police dog that was a beagle hound! I thought this would be an entertaining story to share with my family and friends.

I grabbed my camera, then wondered if there were any laws against taking pictures of police officers or their cuddly police dogs in China. As my mind weighed the options of having proof of this beagle hound or potentially breaking international law, this cuddly dog stuck his nose up in the air, signaling he was onto something. I thought, "Oh wow, we are going to see it in action! Was someone illegally carrying weapons into the country? No, probably drugs. Oh my goodness, did we fly on a plane with a drug lord? That will be an interesting story to tell later!" As he sniffed, he inched closer and closer to us. With each step he took in our direction, the lump in my throat grew larger. Was this the beginning of an unlikely scenario where I would die a tragic and unexpected death while locked up abroad? Control-freak Veronica spiraled.

The policeman now stood in front of us. Something like a game of charades began. He motioned for us to lay our suitcases down, unzip them, and step back. That cute little beagle hound was now the reason I was going to end up in a Chinese prison! Had someone snuck something into our bags unexpectedly? I thought of one of my friends who told me a story about her aunt's best friend's cousin's teacher who had that happen while traveling abroad. The beagle sniffed while the police officer rummaged through our belongings. After what seemed like an eternity, the search stopped. The policeman grabbed a bag of beef jerky, the scented reason for the search, held it up in the air, and said, "For me." A Chinese policeman, with the help of his floppy-eared sidekick, stole our precious beef jerky!

The range of emotions I had just felt was vast—nervousness, excitement, amusement, worry, fear, and terror. Now that we would not end up in a Chinese prison, I was at liberty to choose my next emotion. Was I going to be irritated at the loss of our treasured American snack, or would I react differently? Ron and I were both relieved. The situation was no longer tense and not about drugs or other illegal items, just beef jerky. We played charades to ask the Chinese policeman for a picture of him, his droopy-eyed beagle, and *my* beef jerky. Then we laughed.

Our Chinese Ambulance Ride

Our second Chinese adventure was more dramatic than the first. I gained an admiration for Ron that is beyond explanation. Though we vowed to be faithful "in sickness and in health" at our wedding, neither of us imagined Ron would someday hold me over a squatty potty in China to assist me with bathroom duties.

This stopover trip to Beijing was shortly after our college graduation. Having yet to start our first full-time jobs, we were budget travelers. Our Olympic experience didn't include seeing actual sporting events. We decided seeing the Olympic Torch would check off the "I've been to the Olympics" box on our bucket list. This way, we wouldn't have to buy tickets to see the actual Olympics. We spent an eight-hour day in the sweltering summer heat chasing down the torch with another random American couple. The Chinese government was extremely close-mouthed about the path of the torch.

We discovered a quiet street that was closed to through traffic with barricades along the sidewalks. We were two of only a few people gathered. After checking, we confirmed the torch would indeed pass by here in a few hours. An Olympic worker brought a sign into the road with the number 386 printed on it. Rumors swirled that this would be one place they would exchange the Olympic torch. We took up residence directly in front of the sign, knowing the crowd would eventually swell.

We were right. Within a few hours, our spacious real estate had turned into an overcrowded sidewalk with elbows pushing in from all sides. The press of the crowd separated us from the other American couple, but that was okay. Ron was a big guy, so the two of us stood our ground, keeping our prized vantage point. The crowd grew louder. There it was. The Olympic torch was coming down the road. Wow, what an adventure! I readied my camera for the incredible Kodak moment. Famous people would exchange a piece of history just steps in front of me.

Then something happened. My body became hot, then cold, then dizzy. With the torch just fifty meters from us, I turned around and said, "Ron, I'm not feeling so . . ." And right there, packed into a crowd like a sardine with the Olympic torch right in front of us, I passed out. Ron caught me before I fell, then picked me up and carried me through the crowd. When I came to, I was in Ron's arms as he was yelling, "Help! Help!"

What followed was the first time we experienced God providing for us in a foreign land when we were completely desperate. Two Chinese grandmas motioned to Ron as they jabbered in a language we couldn't comprehend. They popped open a camping stool and sat me down. One poured water on my head while the other fanned me. I thanked them by throwing up on their feet. They chattered some more at Ron. One held a tiny bag with Chinese writing on it. Then suddenly, the grandma ripped open the bag and poured its contents into my mouth—little pills that looked like BBs. The other shoved a water bottle at me, so naturally, I swallowed the pills. My husband looked on in terror. After vomiting and welcoming who-knows-what kind of pills into my digestive system, I felt like my body was about to engage the rear outlet. I needed a bathroom—*fast!*

I told Ron we had to find a bathroom immediately, or he would be stuck in Beijing with a very stinky wife.

Grabbing our Chinese-English dictionary (that was part of my packing frenzy), Ron flipped to the word "toilet." He pointed to the word, hoping these old Chinese grandmas (who now smelled like my vomit) could read it.

At that moment, an English-speaking Olympic worker appeared. After fifteen minutes of chaos with Chinese senior citizens, we were *very* thankful to hear our own language. Ron threw our book bag on his back, picked me up like a baby, and followed this lady to the hospital (apparently the closest bathroom). When we arrived, Ron carried me all the way into the women's restroom to help me get on the toilet. I was still weak and needed assistance. But when we opened the door, there was no toilet, just a squatty potty. We had been out of the US all of six days at this point, so squatting over a pot was not a skill we had acquired yet.

After a quick peek in the other stalls, Ron confirmed I would have to do my business over a squatty potty, even though I was not capable of standing by myself. I looked into Ron's eyes and said, "I can't do this by myself. Will you hold me up?" In an act of self-sacrifice, Ron held me over the hospital squatty potty. Did he not think through what saying yes to this question would mean? Or did he truly love me so much he was willing to be right *there* during *that*? I don't know. Luckily, neither of us found out.

After all that, I couldn't even go. What a dramatic five minutes—all for nothing.

Ron dressed me and helped me to the lobby. The hospital was empty, aside from a group of nurses and a few security guards. Though I was already feeling better, they brought out a gurney and insisted I lie down. Lying on a gurney in the lobby of a Chinese hospital was not the Olympic experience I'd expected, but there was a sense of calm that was very refreshing. The air-conditioning, paired with a soft place to lie, was just what my severely dehydrated body needed.

As we prepared to find a cab and get back to our hotel, the staff insisted we stay longer and take pictures together . . . many, many pictures. My favorite photo was the one of a security guard insisting Ron (who doesn't like to be the center of attention) flex his arm while the security guard felt it. Our Olympic worker friend, still our only translator, told us Ron's "big muscles" impressed the security guard. It amazed him that Ron carried me all the way there.

After our photo op ended, they started rolling my bed. I was still in it. They had called an ambulance to take us back to our hotel. They were worried a cab ride would take too long in all the Olympic traffic. We reluctantly loaded into the ambulance, feeling humbled and also a bit embarrassed by the celebrity-style treatment. The doors shut. Ron looked at me and said, "Look sick." And we laughed.

Dumb and Dumber

Living outside your home culture creates a kind of stress that's hard to explain. We run into so many strange scenarios. Laughing about them is the key to defusing frustrations and staying put until the Lord moves us to our next post. But every expat also has "beef jerky" situations that are nowhere near as amusing. In the aftermath of a tough situation, we ask ourselves, "Can we tell this story in a way that makes us laugh?" Laughing as we go keeps us joyful on the journey. That joy goes a long way. On bad days, finding joy in the bizarre helps us stay in God's will and not flee.

Our days of teaching in South Korea and traveling in East Asia are in the past, but the skills we gained during our time there benefit us today. Currently, our family works among an unreached people group. We focus on evangelism because there are no believers to disciple. Early on, it was exhilarating to use a foreign language to share about the God of the universe creating a path for salvation. But after about ninety rejections, the novelty wore off. How many times we'd endured hearing, "No, that's not true. God didn't do that."

Sometimes when we share, the conversation goes well—maybe 5 percent of the time. About 80 percent of the time, when we speak of the gospel to someone, there isn't much of a discussion. The remaining 15 percent of exchanges are exhausting back and forth. Sometimes, when we try to steer a crazy conversation back to Jesus, we don't even know what to say. Our training didn't teach us how to react when our friend said, "My mom died because someone cursed her. They put a bird in her breast." This is a true story. I spent twenty minutes trying to find out what she meant by "bird in the breast." Was it an idiom for cancer or something else? But my friend insisted, "No. It was a real, live bird." Where was this conversation going? How could I transition from birds lodged in body parts to the gospel and truths of Scripture? It is mental gymnastics to the max, trying to steer a lost person to the feet of the Savior in a foreign language.

What are we to do when birds and breasts are topics of conversation rather than the cross and the resurrection? How do we stay in these relationships and stay in this place where we've been called, despite the many situations and conversations that make our heads spin? How? We laugh.

Ron and I have a code phrase when conversations don't go as planned. I have to confess; this was Ron's idea, not mine. Being a fan of movies that are mind numbingly juvenile, Ron has watched *Dumb and Dumber* a thousand times. In one scene, Lloyd Christmas walks out of a gas station and notices some guys with drinks. Trying to connect with them, he points out their Big Gulps. The reaction he receives is awkward enough to make anyone want to disappear, and so he does.

Early on in our ministry here, Ron and I went to the mall to share the gospel. He had a conversation that was awkward enough to remind him of that *Dumb and Dumber* scene. When I asked him how the conversation went, his response was, "Oh, Big Gulps, huh? Alright! Welp, see ya later!" I immediately burst out laughing. The feeling of tension melted, and we moved on with joy. A *Dumb and Dumber* quote said it all. Ron's feelings were otherwise hard to fully describe.

When life takes you overseas, you have to be prepared to laugh, mainly at yourself. As children, our parents trained us to follow cultural norms in our passport country. They taught us to sit properly at the table, chew with our mouths closed, and say please and thank you. When we landed overseas, we realized the cultural norms and habits we were accustomed to were no longer relevant. Sit properly at the table? People here sit on the floor while dining. Chew with your mouth closed? Hosts here are too vivacious to finish chewing before they interject. Say please and thank you? There isn't even a great way to express "please" in our host culture. When missionaries land in a new country aiming to push back darkness, life can feel awkward, scary, and lonely. How do we deal with these overwhelming feelings while also adapting to hotter environments, new food, and long walking distances? We laugh. We take every opportunity we can to laugh. Because through that, joy germinates and grows.

Every hero of the faith persevered through hard stuff. And not just big, hard events like deaths and hospitalizations but also everyday irritations, including those that come with living life overseas. These challenges build character and shape us for the future. As we become more resilient, our resolve to stay strengthens. When we're offended, confused, or unable to live like we want, it's easy to feel frustrated, but can we find a way to laugh about it and dodge the devil's daggers? Our answer to that determines whether we will stay or flee.

Ride 'em Cowgirl

When Adventure Kicks In

The Cowgirl in Me

Before we left for the mission field, our coworkers voted us "Most Likely to End Up on the Amazing Race." We were in a room with other missionaries who would soon move to places so remote my geography knowledge failed me. The nomination surprised me, but after a few years overseas, it made sense. The thrill seeker in me, paired with Ron's laid-back, always-game personality, often landed us in strange situations. Adventure is something we both enjoy. If I'm doing something that makes no sense, it's because I'm in a good place in my heart and have decided to carpe diem. I'll probably end up like my grandma, jumping out of a plane at eighty-seven.

If I weren't a missionary, I would be a trick rider at the Dixie Stampede. By the time I was two years old, my dad had me riding horses. Dad's cousin gave Dad two horses that year—one for my older sister and one for Dad. The backside of Dad's horse was for me. I rode double with my dad for so many hours that my legs might well have bowed like a true cowgirl. Paired with my love for anything horseback was a love for gymnastics. In fourth grade, my mom grew fed up with me vaulting over the living room couch and enrolled me in gymnastics class. It was a good attempt on her part to redirect poor behavior. But after a few years of gymnastics, vaulting over the couch turned into attempts at vaulting onto my horse. My two passions collided.

We had the sweetest horse—an Arabian-Saddlebred mix. This breeding combination typically results in a dynamite personality—a temperament capable of exploding at any moment. Ami, however, was delightfully different. God must have made her with me in mind. She was the calmest, most patient babysitter horse ever. I spent hours riding her bareback. I'd stand on her bottom and do somersaults to her neck. When she galloped under a tree, I'd attempt a running dismount by grabbing a limb and sliding off. I even learned to ride standing up on her back. I'd get her walking or trotting, then pull my legs up to her back and slowly stand up. As my confidence grew, I was determined to learn how to stand up while she galloped. However, being an excellent babysitter, Ami knew better. The minute I pulled my legs up while she was in a gallop, she would slow back down to a trot. I'm sure she was thinking, "This crazy child will not die on my watch!"

Every spring and fall, my dad took me to southern Illinois with a group of his friends. I would take a few days off from school to ride horses with them in the Shawnee National Forest. We would leave camp early and ride the entire day. It was normally a ten-hour day in the saddle. I can still close my eyes and feel the muscles of my horse tighten as she lunged up the rocky bluffs in the rain. I remember the sweet scent of fall as we crossed a creek through a narrow valley with cliffs on both sides. By that point, no one could deny I was a certified cowgirl.

A Not-So-Trusty Steed

While we've had our fair share of once-in-a-lifetime events, there is one that tops them all. After teaching in Korea for a year, we prepared to return to the US. On our way back, we scheduled a ten-day mission trip because adventure awaited! During that trip, my cowgirl skills and spirit were tested. There's a certain amount of pride a cowgirl (or cowboy) has in their ability to control a one-thousand-pound animal. There isn't much I'd be afraid to do if I had a dependable horse underneath me (the key word here is dependable). This bravado gets many cowgirls and cowboys into trouble.

One day on our ten-day mission trip, we went to a village to connect with a family that lived there. We ate strange food while sitting in a sweltering house with the sweetest group of people. We understood none of what they were saying or doing. Because we were in a new country on our way back to the United States from Korea, our language learning in those ten days amounted to "Hello" and "How are you?" Our missionary hosts attempted to translate as much as possible, but the natural flow of conversation limited how much they could comment.

One thing the missionary made sure to translate was news of a new ostrich farm down the road. I guess he thought since ostriches and horses both have legs, naturally, I would be interested. He'd told the family I was an expert horseman. They looked at me expectantly. As a cowgirl, there was only one way to respond to this ostrich farm story. I cleared my throat and smiled, "Well, if I can ride a horse, I can ride an ostrich."

After an hour or two of eating, laughing, and (on our end) not understanding anything, everyone packed up their things. The women took the food from the table, put it together like a picnic, and carried it to the car. "Interesting," I thought. "Maybe they're going to the beach. Maybe they're going to another party and taking the leftovers." I asked our missionary hosts what was happening. He responded, "We're going to the ostrich farm so you can ride an ostrich."

What! Panic set in. Ride an ostrich? A real live, moving ostrich? Oh my goodness! We were at least two hours from a hospital that resembled anything in the modern world. Veronica! Why did you open your mouth? Why do you get yourself into such predicaments?

We loaded into our friends' truck. Sweat from the heat mixed with sweat from my fear. I was frazzled. I mentally ran to my place of safety while sitting in the truck. My conversation with God went something like this: "God, what on earth was I thinking? This is a horrible idea. If I don't ride this dumb ostrich, I'm going to disappoint the caravan of people expecting to see an American cowgirl bestride a bird-beast. On the other hand, WHO ON EARTH RIDES AN OSTRICH? This can't be safe. Lord, You've never let me down. I know I tend to test You with my constant antics, but would You please be with me through this one too? This is the worst idea I've ever had. I need assurance. How about this? I think three things need to happen for me to ride an ostrich safely in the middle of nowhere. If

You meet all these conditions, I'll trust You're telling me I'll be okay. If not, I'll use that as an excuse to back out. Okay? Yes, this is a good way to do it. Okay, Lord. First, it must be a tame ostrich—or at least as tame as an enormous bird creature can be. It needs to be accustomed to people. Second, the ostrich should be in a pen. I don't want it to run off down the road, forcing me to bail out into a ditch where there could be an alligator. Finally, someone has to have ridden the ostrich previously. Lord, I'd love to have an excuse not to ride this ostrich, but Your will be done. If this is a piece of the puzzle You'll use for this family to hear the gospel, then I guess not even an ostrich should stand in the way."

After these conditions were clear in my mind, I somehow attained peace while bumping down the dirt roads that led to the ostrich farm. As we arrived and unloaded, excitement was in the air. Old grandmas and aunties chattered at me with smiles on their faces and grabbed me for photos. The time had come. We walked into the farm.

A nice, middle-aged woman met us. She told me the name of the ostrich I would ride and shared how she had raised it from birth. Uh-oh. I checked the first condition off my list. After a brief walk, we arrived at their fenced arena, complete with rickety "grandstands." Ugh. Condition number two—met. Finally, this sweet lady walked me over to the fence and told me she would show me how to ride the ostrich first, then I would go. Oh no. She'd satisfied all three of my conditions. I had to ride the ostrich.

My stomach churned as I watched the lady walk up to a triangle-shaped "chute" to mount her magnificent steed. After mounting the giant bird, she bounced around the arena, holding its wings. Her husband ran on the ground to help shoo it in the direction he thought it should go. Then, halfway through the ride, the ostrich stepped right, she leaned left, and off she tumbled to the ground. With that dramatic, unplanned dismount, it was my turn.

I walked into the arena to the triangular chute. The man had corralled the ostrich back inside it after putting a sock on the bird's head. "Probably so it doesn't peck me to death," I thought. I mounted the bird-beast and waited, frozen in the chute. I imagined my feelings were like those of my contemporaries in the US who go into chutes to mount wild horses and bulls in rodeos. How did I arrive at this place? I posed for a few quick pictures, my stomach in knots. Then with a "1-2-3-GO!" off the bird went. Its gait was unfamiliar, hopping sporadically from here to there. Its feather-covered skin wasn't smooth like my Arabian horse. Instead, similar in composition to some reptile, its skin shed then stuck in flakes onto my sweaty legs. There were no reins to hold, just the collapsing neck of this beast. We hopped here and there. Nothing felt familiar, but after a few minutes, I realized I probably wouldn't die and settled into the experience.

How did I arrive at that moment? I'm still not sure, but it had something to do with wanting to immerse myself in the unknown of a new place—exploration and adventure. When I realized I would not die on that ostrich, a rush of excitement shot through me. I was connecting to a new culture in a crazy way. That memory will stick with me until my mind no longer functions. After a blurry ten-minute ride, I conquered the ostrich challenge. The owners of the farm corralled my not-so-trusty steed back to the chute, and I dismounted without incident. Adventure had called, and I was a willing participant. My heart felt fresh. I was excited to engage with all that was new in that place.

Wedding Crashers
Several years later, we followed the Lord's call and moved to the "Land of the Ostrich." During the first year or two there, we eagerly absorbed the culture and engaged with our community. New food, new sites, new sounds—it was all so fresh. We wanted to learn everything about the Land of the Ostrich so we would know how to share the gospel with the people. Without an understanding of the

culture, it would be impossible to find effective ways to share about Jesus.

We spent a year learning the language in a nearby city before moving to our host city. The first week we lived in the Land of the Ostrich was a holiday week. I attended a party (of sorts) at a local mall. Music blared, but I managed to share the gospel with the stranger sitting next to me. Although I couldn't make out her response, my heart swelled with joy. I could feel it in my soul. I was born for this. The goodbyes with my sweet pup and our families and the liquidation of my American life were for this—so *this* woman and her family would hear of God's love for them and the way to salvation. A friendship between the two of us began that day.

I soon learned my new friend was a wedding coordinator in a low-income housing area. The population was at least ten thousand people, and 99.9 percent of them were lost—most had never even heard the name of Jesus. This began a period in our lives when we (and many of our friends) called ourselves "wedding crashers," because that's basically what we did for a living. Weddings were our gateway to the community and opportunities for conversation and sharing the gospel.

One might imagine us sitting in a church in nice Sunday clothes with a different family every week; however, that isn't the type of activity I'm talking about. The events we attended were more like wedding receptions. Before each wedding, our friend told us the bride's theme color. Guests were supposed to wear that color. On most occasions, we did not have the customary clothes that were the right color, so we would buy a cheap traditional outfit or borrow something to wear from our friends. My favorite one was a 1980s-style yellow ball gown I borrowed, complete with puffy sleeves and a heart-shaped neckline. We arrived at these weddings looking like people who both belonged, yet did not belong. We wore the right color clothes, but our skin color was different.

Most weddings took place outside under a canopy on the partially paved roads of the complex. The smell of trash, compounded by the scorching heat of day, wafted in the air. A DJ would play music, and often a group of singers would sing to the music played by the DJ. The volume of music was loud enough to burst eardrums. Each event started around noon and sometimes continued for several days, depending on the couple's budget. We'd usually arrive around three o'clock when the day's heat was fading. And we would stay until our brains wore out—when we could no longer handle communication in a foreign language.

Upon arrival, someone would parade us into the reception and up to the front to meet the bride and groom. The couple would look at us with terrified expressions on their faces, likely trying to remember how to say "nice to meet you" in English. Ron would crack a joke in their language so they would relax and speak freely to us. Then a photo session would begin. The bride, groom, and their families would file to the front to get their pictures taken with the Americans as if we were an exhibit at the zoo. After the photo op, someone would escort us to the line to fill up on local food, and we would sit down to eat. While dining, we'd try to strike up conversations with the people around us over the loud music.

At sundown, singers would arrive, or, if they were already there, they would change their clothes. During the day, their clothes were very modest—their heads might even be covered. But a weird thing happened at night. When the sun went down, so did the square footage of fabric on their bodies. They replaced their draping skirts with fishnet tights and their loose, long-sleeve shirts with corset tops. Their head coverings were most often replaced with live pythons! That's right. Of course, the first time we experienced this new post-sundown culture, we were with an older American couple who were in town volunteering with us. We took them to the wedding without imagining we would see yellow pythons and fishnet hosiery.

That night, our brains persisted longer than they normally did (maybe because we had more breaks to speak

English with our friends). Time flew by, and the sun went down. Suddenly, parts of the singers' clothes disappeared. Then they pulled the tablecloth off one of the tables in the front, and ta-dah! Under this table in a clear plastic box was a large, yellow python. Next to it was its snake friend, but he was greenish brown. Two pythons had apparently hung out with us for much of the reception. If I were thinking of ways to store a python, a plastic box made for Christmas decorations wouldn't be what I'd use. We were mortified we'd brought volunteers to this type of event, albeit unknowingly. However, to our surprise, the couple easily laughed off the unexpected situation.

The husband marched up to the front for a photo next to the people holding the python. No way was I going to translate for him! Now alone in the front of the building with around three hundred onlookers, he stood while ladies proceeded to load the python onto his neck. That wedding crashing adventure was a very interesting and unexpected learning experience. We didn't stay long after sundown, but we used what we saw to ask people new questions about their culture, sin, and forgiveness. If we hadn't taken the chance to learn and be adventurous, we wouldn't have gained that insight into the culture. To be clear, we prefer fully clothed settings. However, my point is the more we know about the culture, the more effective we can be in our work.

While this might not sound like a fun Friday night, it overjoyed us to be there. We laughed at how ridiculous we looked arriving at each event. We loved trying new foods. (Though after one round of me asking, "What's this?" about each dish, Ron requested I stop. He preferred to pretend it was all just chicken and potatoes.) Most of all, we enjoyed connecting with new people and sharing the story that would connect them back to their Creator.

Our relationship with Cathy, the wedding planner we met at the mall, was a win-win. While I don't enjoy my nationality or skin color being used in a relationship for someone else's benefit, it opened doors for the gospel to go into that low-income housing area. Over the course of two years, we shared the gospel and watched *The Jesus Film* with many families in that complex. Adventure took us there. The gospel kept us there.

When Adventure Calls

During our early years overseas, we found the Land of the Ostrich fascinating and exhilarating. We didn't notice the rats in the street because the neon signs in a new language diverted our attention. Without thinking about what might come afterward, we tried new foods and flavors. We'd chalk up the resulting "tummy bugs" to getting used to the place. It was all so mesmerizing. We dove into situations that were fresh and adventurous because our hearts were eager to engage the people. Nasty (to us) foods and strange traditions were what we expected when we came overseas. The honeymoon phase of our move lasted one to two years. We felt like God made us for this place and this job. But eventually, the newness of the spices and street signs wore off, and the rats and stomach bugs became more apparent.

But God called us to this place, and our calling is what keeps us here. Just like a marriage, the beginning of life on the field is exciting. As time passes, the allure of life abroad can fade. Certain things about it annoy us. So how do missionaries stay for the long haul? We remember why we fell in love with our location.

If someone is thinking about moving abroad for ministry, I would say when you're in the "falling in love" phase, take pictures and keep a journal. Write down the stories that made your heart grow fond of your new country. Take videos of your first drive, your first home, your first time cooking. Then down the road, just as one might do on the bad days of a marriage, think about the beginning. Ask yourself why you came to begin with. What endeared you to the area? In my mind, God gives us this season of falling in love with a place so we can pin it in our minds and come back to it on the bad days. So don't forget the beginning. It might just be what helps you stay—and not flee—on a bad day.

CHAPTER 4

Lost in Translation

When My Hair and Dignity Vanished

A word of warning—the stories in this chapter may change your impression of me. These are stories we swap with expats for laughs and one-ups but hesitate to share with supporters back in the States. However, for the sake of explaining how humbling life abroad can be, I'm going to lay bare my most embarrassing moments.

Lost Hair
One day in heaven, I will ask God why He gave me the hair He did. I'm not vain—I was the cheerleader my college teammates constantly reprimanded for not primping well enough. My hair question for God is more

a matter of my precious time on this planet and less a matter of my appearance.

After nearly forty years of life, I've yet to find a way to cut and style my hair so I can get out of bed and do very little before leaving. Maybe God would say the bigger problem is my impatience and my unwillingness to invest over five minutes in a morning beauty routine. Regardless, my poor hair stays in a sad state most of the time because I don't care enough to style it.

While living in Korea, beauty was a constant topic. My poor country-girl heart struggled to connect with people who prided themselves on physical appearance. But there was a hairstyle I eyed the entire year we were in Korea. My principal had this beautiful, loose wavy perm. I'd had perms in the past, so I thought if my hair could achieve that same look, I'd be able to get ready in less than five minutes. I could shower, scrunch some styling spray in my hair, and walk out the door. I coveted the thought—not so much the hair, but the time that hairstyle would save me.

For nearly a year in Korea, I let my hair grow so it would be long enough for a perm and ponytail. Finally, a month prior to leaving Korea, I decided it was time to pull the trigger. I would go to a reputable salon with excellent hair stylists. My Korean friend would come along to translate what I wanted, and *voila!* For the next six months, I would have the coveted five-minute hairdo.

One day after school, we went to the hair salon. I had already explained to my coworker, Trisha, exactly what I wanted. That was easy enough, considering it was our principal's hairdo—that's what I wanted. This was before cell phones had cameras. However, I had no worries. I trusted Trisha to translate.

When we arrived, and Trisha began explaining, it appeared the ladies didn't quite understand what I wanted. On a whim, I pointed at a short-haired woman in the shop and said, "Like that! I want my curls to be about that size, but the length to be like it is now." Trisha, who was completely fluent in Korean, translated. I have no idea what was *actually* said, but the ladies saw who I pointed to, and apparently their brains settled there. I sat down in the chair, assuming they would begin right away with rollers.

A lady with one good eye and one lazy eye came to my chair. It surprised me that this woman was a hairdresser because, after all, cutting hair requires the ability to see. But I figured, "No big deal, she doesn't need to see well to put in the rollers. That's probably her specialty." Then it happened—the noise that shattered my hair dreams. *Chop!* I quickly asked Trisha, who was talking to someone else, what the chopping noise was. She turned and sheepishly responded, "Uh, Veronica, bad news. They cut your hair like *that* lady's hair." She motioned toward the woman I had pointed to. I sat in disbelief. The lady with only one good eye had cut off seven inches of my hair! Seven inches of hair that took me ten months to grow long enough to achieve the level of laziness I desperately desired—the means to primp myself quickly for the day. That *chop* not only significantly shortened my hair, but it also chopped off my dream. And there went my ponytail. How could I possibly handle life without the ability to have a ponytail?

Even after this mishap, I let her proceed to the perm. I should have taken the disastrous haircut as a sign to stop, but I didn't. Because my hair was now very short, the big rollers no longer fit. They had to use small rollers. The appointment was one tragic blow after another. When I finally walked out of the salon, I looked like I had stuck my finger in a light socket. Really. Imagine the most horrid perm from the eighties. That was on my head. Except it wasn't the eighties, and poodle perms were no longer in style. I'm not a girl that typically worries about a bad haircut. Generally, my motto is "Hair grows out. Try something adventurous!" But at this point in life, I was a lazy American farm girl living in a place that prioritized beauty. Not only was my chance at a five-minute morning routine shot, but I also looked like

Michael Jackson. When I got home, I immediately jumped in the shower to rinse out as much of the perm as I could. As I washed my hair, I noticed the hair stylist had missed cutting large sections of my hair. I guess that's what I get for hiring a hairstylist with one good eye. My new 'do was mostly chin-length hair with random sections of longer hair. Twelve hours later, I stood in front of a snickering high school class with my disastrous haircut. They commented. It was embarrassing.

God taught me a very simple lesson about life overseas that day: hold on to my plans (and my dignity) loosely. Things get lost in translation, like hair. I can't allow small, eternally insignificant things to become big things in my heart.

Lost Dignity

Language school is a precious gift to an expat. But it's also grueling. It's like attempting to fill buckets of water in a tropical storm.

LANGUAGE SCHOOL TEACHER. Hunker down, everyone! Information overload is incoming!" *Whooosshh!* "Did anyone catch anything? Are you alive?! Where did your bucket go?"
LANGUAGE SCHOOL STUDENT. Did I catch anything? I don't even know what my name is anymore."

Imagine the typical idiom, "It's like drinking from a firehose." Then multiply the water pressure by fifteen and visualize being held upside down and spun around. That's a glimpse of immersive language learning in a foreign place.

Although it's totally exhausting, wow, is it worth it! Without a good command of the language, we'd basically be running around like the Tower of Babel just happened. Our time in Korea had many comparable moments. The school we taught at wouldn't allow students to speak Korean during the day, even if it was to help coach their American teachers. Our dreams of learning some Korean while living in Korea came crashing down with that revelation. We ended up playing charades and saying English words in a Korean accent to communicate outside of school.

Despite the language barrier, we lived normally in Korea. Our church service was in English. Our school day was in English. All our friends spoke English. Our family doctor spoke *enough* English. The only challenging moments were with strangers. Most of the time, our English spoken in a Korean accent plus the charades game got us through just fine. But there was one very embarrassing day when our communication efforts were insufficient.

Street food didn't sit well with my stomach the year we were in Korea. Apparently, I have zero tolerance for

TO STAY OR FLEE

amoebas and other random foodborne germs. This is another question I plan to ask God when I reach heaven. Did He forget when He made my body that I'd be living in multiple foreign countries? Or was Paul's thorn in the flesh also a stomach that could not tolerate street food? Whatever the answer, after ten months of street food, I needed to see a gastroenterologist. Most of our doctor's appointments were scheduled through the counselor at our school or a fellow teacher who could help us navigate the hospitals. Someone usually went to the hospital with us to help with registration and introduce us to the doctor. However, this wasn't an appointment I wanted to share with my boss, or anyone really. I was a new expat, embarrassed to be a twenty-something headed to the gastroenterologist. Ron and I scheduled an appointment on our own. We would leave Korea in a week, but because we would be transferring to a new health insurance provider back home, I needed a diagnosis before we switched to ensure coverage. Plus, I was losing weight rapidly. We assumed the doctor would speak English, as that had always been the case. We'd be fine.

When we arrived, we found the specialist hospital not as foreigner-friendly as expected. Navigating the check-in procedures and paperwork was difficult. However, when the doctor came in for my exam, it was exactly as we had willed it to be. His English was perfect. He was knowledgeable. This was going to be fine. After the initial consultation, the physician sent me upstairs to meet with another doctor. When I arrived, several nurses came to help me. Ron and I had no idea what was going on. They kept saying this weird word we couldn't understand. I went through a strange process. (I now know the English term for it is an *enema*.)

The nurses then began pointing to their watches, signing the number five, and pointing out the door. I was uncomfortable, confused, and embarrassed. None of what they were signing or saying made any sense to me. A nurse led me to the bathroom and continued pointing at her watch. She showed me the number five with her hand. Ron and I played detective, trying to figure out what those poor nurses were trying to tell us. We are generally competent people, but I've noticed when we encounter a vast cultural difference or feel pressured to communicate in a language we don't speak, it's like our brains cease to operate.

As we sat in the waiting room, trying to figure out what was happening, *it* happened. My stomach gurgled, and I ran for the bathroom. But the toilet was too far. Luckily, I was wearing hospital pants instead of my own pants. Suffice it to say, the hospital had a stinky cleanup job, thanks to my lack of language proficiency. Those poor nurses were trying to tell me they had given me an enema and that I would need to be in the bathroom in five minutes, or . . . well, *this* would happen. This is one of the most embarrassing moments of my life. As a twenty-something, going to a gastroenterologist is humiliating. Finding out you're about to have a colonoscopy is horrifying. And, well, pooping your pants before your first colonoscopy? I don't have the words.

After Ron helped me clean up from the bathroom nightmare, I prepared for my first colonoscopy, which would take place in a foreign country. Now that I knew what was happening, I was in full freak-out mode. No one spoke English. Did I mention I was a twenty-something? I knew nothing about colonoscopies. I was ready to put my pants back on and leave the hospital! If this bathroom episode was a precursor for what was to come, I was *not* interested!

Thankfully, after this mishap, a nice English-speaking doctor came to get me in the waiting room. He must have felt bad that I was too young and ignorant to understand the word enema spoken with a Korean accent. He described the procedure and thoroughly answered my questions. With an exhale and a prayer, "Thank You, Lord, for doctors around the world who speak English," my first colonoscopy began. The rest of the procedure went smoothly. The doctor was super helpful, forewarning me of what I might feel and teaching me trivia about the human intestine. "Look see that's your..." Barf. I didn't want to know. But he must have thought since the word enema was lost in translation, he should give me a play-by-play to make up for it. The colonoscopy ended. I dressed. Then the doctor brought out a vial of some liquid and a biopsy of my colon to take back to the US. I was gifted a vial with a piece of my intestine in it. What do you even do with that? Well, I put the little container in a plastic sack and walked home—as if the piece of my intestine was some pudding I had just purchased from Walmart.

Living overseas offers a lot of opportunities for embarrassment. We dive into situations daily that are...well, foreign. Some of these situations end well. Some end with you pooping your pants in a Korean hospital. I'd prefer to skip those experiences. Being humiliated is part of life overseas. Not that it happens all the time, but it will happen. How do we react in these moments of frustration so that we stay overseas for the long haul? We allow God to use them to develop a heart of humility in us. I mean, nothing kicks pride to the curb like pooping your pants, right? If you expect to always have it together, you're going to miss opportunities to learn from refining moments. It's kind of like middle school. No one wants to be laughed at, but hopefully we develop the character to endure embarrassing moments and insults. An experience like that isn't fun, but it will refine and strengthen who we're becoming.

Lost My Mind

The second time we moved overseas, our organization gave us the gift of language classes. It was a requirement, but I call it a gift because it *was* a gift. The consequences of not knowing the language in Korea were...well, I've already shared stories. So yes, it was a gift. Upon arrival, we began our time in a landing city for language school. It was an *amazing* city—trendy, mountainous, and breathtakingly beautiful. It was full of life and warm, welcoming people. Clothes, movies, and travel were all cheap. We had no expectations when we moved because we would only stay there until we had a handle on the language. Oh, but did we fall in *love*!

In my expat years, I've come to adore places around the world where the sensation of our plane's wheels hitting the runway feels like turning onto my grandma's road at Christmas. It feels like home. This city is one of those places. Whenever I return, my heart delights in all the sounds, smells, and sights as I disembark from the plane. This place! God took a piece of my heart and left it here. Not in a theological way, but in a this-place-is-now-a-part-of-me kind of way.

Although I'm not a third-culture kid (TCK), my children are, and I can already see them developing the same feelings. Certain restaurants or places in cities we might pass through every two years trigger a different demeanor. Smiles warmly spread across their faces. Their bodies relax. This is a part of their complex home.

It's hard for an expat or TCK to recreate foods or explain an affection for foreign cities and traditions when they return to their passport country. People have written books on the complexity of the matter. For the expat, and especially the TCK, home is complicated and can't be described. It's the foreign city where we live and work. It's back in our passport country, which can feel like a foreign place (especially for a TCK). It's nowhere. It's everywhere. But ultimately, home is living together in the place God has called us to as a family.

That language city soon became our home. Our hearts latched onto the people there. We shared meals and amoebas, laughter and heartache. And we learned the language. Part of why we were so enamored with that place was the feeling of "growing up" there. When we arrived, we only knew the word "Hi." We couldn't experience anything deeply because everything was incomprehensible. But, in a few short months, we grew from language infants to language toddlers. Then, a few months later, we were adolescents who could share most of our minds and hearts with any local who walked by.

Ron and I love to explore. During the first few weeks of language school, we had to memorize a 3–4 sentence script about ourselves for conversation practice. We were supposed to go to a mall or wherever people gathered to say our script to at least three people a day. The next day, we would be held accountable by sharing our experiences with our class. Who did we meet? What did we learn about that person? The first few days, we went to the mall closest to our language school. Day one was okay. However, on days two and three, we ended up reintroducing ourselves to the same people we met on day one. Well, that was embarrassing and (am I allowed to say this?) boring. We could only say three or four sentences, and, because we couldn't understand anything, it was an awkward conversation.

ME. Hi, I'm Veronica. I am married. I'm from America.

RANDOM MALL WORKER, *replies quickly in a language I don't understand.*

ME, *smiling big, hoping this person doesn't think I'm rude.* Uh . . . Okay, bye!

By the second or third week of language school, we had figured out a better system. We would look on

Tripadvisor for a cool restaurant, mall, or sightseeing spot and determine the general direction using Google Maps. Then, instead of taking a map or GPS with us, we'd navigate to the place solely by speaking the language (yes, the language of which we knew fifteen words). To check off our homework, we would introduce ourselves to 2–3 people when we arrived.

To navigate to a target location, we would generally pull our car over about a block before a big intersection, yell at a random person walking down the street, and say something like, "Hi! Where is volcano?" The person would answer with a fast, "Turn this way, go straight, turn that way, and you're there." Ron and I would thank this stranger, roll up our window, and debate whether we heard left, right, or straight first. After we formed a consensus, we would drive in that direction maybe a quarter mile down the road and repeat the process.

This city was not Small Town, USA. It was the size of LA. We weren't navigating across a quaint little town. We were navigating through streets jam-packed with thousands of people and cars. Imagine two fresh foreigners in their car creeping up to people in LA and using broken English to ask for directions. In America, a neighborhood watch would probably report us to the police. But in this warm, welcoming culture, the people happily assisted us along our language-learning journey each day. We loved practicing this way. It kept our daily experiences fresh enough that language learning didn't feel monotonous. It also gave us an opportunity to be tourists. Maybe that was part of the reason we fell in love with the city so quickly.

While out on our daily field trips, we would notice common signs across town. Being curious language learners, we often discussed these with one another and friends. One such sign had us confused even after a month or two of language study. Here's the thing. There are two levels to learning a language. There's what each word means. And what each word *means*. Sometimes two or more words are grouped together to form an idiom. Other times, pop culture changes a straightforward word into a word with a very different meaning in context.

After numerous drives across town, one sign had us stumped. "MEDICINE STRONG." Ron and I discussed what this sign might mean and why it seemed to be *everywhere*. We asked the brightest language student in our class. He had been in the country for a full three months. Of course, he would know. But he had no answer. Then, one day in class, we finished a lesson early. My brain had hit a delirious language-learning haze. I mentioned the mysterious sign after class to eight of our peers. No one knew, not even our Korean classmate. That had us really perplexed because he seemed to know more vocabulary than the dictionary. Now the rest of our class was with us on the quest to learn why the medicine was so strong. (I say they were with us, but I was probably most motivated to find the answer.)

Our innocent instructor was only two months into his job teaching his language to foreigners. The more seasoned teachers had been through so many rounds of language school; they practically knew American culture better than we did. They could answer questions in a way our Western brains understood and absorbed. In a worst-case scenario, they could always flip over to English. But poor Mr. Sams—he could not. He spoke no English and had no command of Western culture to explain things from our perspective. And he was incredibly shy. In the downtime lag that day, I did what any inquisitive language learner would do.

ME. Mr. Sams, I see sign says, "Medicine Strong." What does it mean?

MR. SAMS, *with a bright red face.* Uh . . . A medicine for men.

ME. If I want. I take?

MR. SAMS, *chuckles nervously.* No.

ME. Why?

MR. SAMS. It's a medicine for men.

Understanding hadn't dawned on me yet. When that line of questioning did not yield a straight answer, I felt my frustration rising. I was determined to sort this out. I tried again, receiving similar answers. Decoding this phrase was essential to fully understanding the language and culture. Therefore, my classmates needed to know this phrase too. I would be the champion of our cause, leading us to successful language and culture learning today! I flipped over to English and discussed Mr. Sam's answers with our class. The only feasible explanation in our minds (as a class of eight missionaries who were *way* too naive to figure this out quickly) was that "Medicine Strong" was a certain type of recreational drug or steroid. In this context, they would not sell it to women for some reason. I felt betrayed as a woman. I mean, not that I think women should do drugs or take steroids, but how oppressive was this culture to not even *allow* women to do that if they wanted? We asked Mr. Sams in English if it was drugs or steroids. He said no. He didn't know enough English to give a true no, I reasoned. I felt we were on the right track but needed more clarification with another teacher because Mr. Sams didn't speak English well enough to confirm our suspicions.

Class dismissed. We went downstairs to the next class. Some of our peers joined, and some went into other classes. A few students came into this new class along with us who had not been in the previous one. Again, I couldn't let it go. For the sake of my curiosity and my peers' learning, I had to know what this was. This time, our teacher was a gregarious veteran who could certainly help. I faced the situation as any other loopy language-learning student who had hit delirium. Still assuming this medicine was steroids or drugs, I raised my hand and made an announcement, using the language I knew.

ME. Mr. Michaels, last night Ron eat Medicine Strong. He go jail.

Mr. Michael's reaction was akin to a scene from Looney Tunes. He stopped in his tracks with big eyes, mouth gaping. By his body language, I could tell that my classmates (who had been drug along on the drug ride) and I still did *not* understand.

MR. MICHAELS. Did Ron really take Medicine Strong?
ME, *in English.* No. I just don't know what this phrase means. I've seen it on signs. Mr. Sams tried to explain, but I—WE don't get it!
MR. MICHAELS, *who is now calm and composed like a true veteran teacher.* It's a medicine for men that makes women happy.

ME. Oh . . . whoops! *Now fully aware that I had said my husband took that medicine.*

Ron loathed me doing this type of thing during language school. I would jump into a conversation, despite not knowing enough vocabulary to converse. Then I would fumble through an uncomfortable discussion and carry everyone in the room along with me. I contest it helped me learn the language faster. Ron said it was embarrassing. Both were true. My crusade to discover the meaning of "Medicine Strong" was our most humiliating venture in Veronica's Language-Learning Campaign. But even in the embarrassment, I was thankful to have the gift of language learning. Imagine saying what I said about my husband and never figuring it out!

Life Lost in Translation
Expat life offers so many opportunities to be humiliated. Maybe it's one way God keeps our egos in check. After almost ten years in the same city, speaking the same foreign language, I still get confused and misunderstand life around me. My understanding is better than it was when we arrived, but since this isn't my home country, I'll never fully understand everything. Perhaps our best response to life getting lost in translation is to remain open to it happening again and again. As we interact

cross-culturally, we will make mistakes. The natural response to embarrassment is to shrink back. When I make a mistake in conversation, and people laugh, I naturally think twice before speaking again. However, if I allow speaking errors to silence me, will I be brave enough to speak the truth of Jesus' love when the time arises? We must let go of our dignity. Missionaries must dive into conversations and be okay with embarrassment. God didn't call me to glorify me. He called me to glorify Himself.

CHAPTER 5

Weathering Storms

When You Don't Have the Expertise or Energy on Your Own

In life, storms loom no matter where we are geographically. When we're in our passport country, gloomy seasons are usually easier to weather because we have a larger support system—family, friends, and fellow church members we know from years of living there. However, how do we handle the hurricanes that hit when we're living overseas? Well, the severity of the damage will most likely correlate to the strength (or lack) of our support system. In my experience, there are four types of people that make up a robust safety net: a local, a colleague, a volunteer from our passport country, and a remote friend or family member I can count on and confide in. The following stories are a snapshot of people in our support system and how they've helped us stay in God's will through storms.

Love from a Local

Ron and I moved overseas before we had children, so we haven't parented fully in our home culture. Yes, we've *visited* our home country and experienced the culture with our children, but we haven't *lived* there with them. There's a difference. We learn about life from the surrounding community, especially parenting. The proverb "It takes a village to raise a child" comes to mind.

When my daughter was 1-2 months old, I remember lamenting to some local friends that my baby wasn't nursing until she was full—just until she fell back asleep. She couldn't take a bottle, so I was constantly up at night. These friends graciously came to my house to help, but their advice was not helpful.

FRIEND. It's ok. Just let her eat. Later if she wakes up, you feed her again.

ME. But then I can't sleep for more than an hour or two at a time. I'm exhausted.

FRIEND. It's ok. Baby will grow and drink more milk. Eventually, she'll be like my three-year-old son and only need a bottle once overnight.

Nursing my baby throughout the night until she was three was not my plan. But a few years after this conversation, I realized where they were coming from. All these sweet ladies giving me guidance had live-in maids who helped take care of their babies. That's why giving a bottle at midnight wasn't a big deal to them like it was to me— a mom with no maid and no family around to help.

Everyone offered opinions about parenting to me early on. That happens to every first-time mother. Some opinions were from family in the US, some were from American colleagues, some were from a very blunt local people group, and some were from a more soft-spoken local people group. If I'd written every opinion or suggestion down on a piece of paper and crossed out the opposing views, I'd have ended with no suggestions at all. I'm not saying anyone was wrong—just that, as a new mom, the conflicting advice was confusing. I had entered a new phase of life, one I hadn't learned in my home culture. Parenting decisions seemed endless. My head spun, trying to determine which options were right for us.

Then God sent us an angel—this woman had to be. That is the only explanation for how kind, patient, and loving our sweet Auntie Cora was. Her ability to exhibit the fruit of the Spirit was beyond anything I thought possible.

We met Auntie Cora before we had kids. She had fled from her wealthy family after becoming a believer. Fancy European vacations and expensive cars were things of her past. Why would someone seek the reverse of a rags-to-riches story? Anyone who shares a short meal with Auntie Cora will understand. She'll say, "My friend, I haven't traded riches for rags. I've traded earthly treasures for Heavenly ones that are *much* more abundant and valuable."

When we met Cora, Ron and I were in the same boat, needing to be cautious about who we shared our full story with. Learning how to be missionaries in a place closed to that kind of work was complicated. Auntie Cora became like a sister to me during that time. We were kindred spirits undercover and "all in" for Jesus.

When my babies came along, Auntie Cora was there for me like a sister. After baby two was born, another new phase began. Ron and I started a business that would give us an identity within the community and more access to the lost. We had no experience in business, so it was overwhelming. Becoming entrepreneurs in a foreign country, doing mission work, and caring for a two-year-old and an infant required more energy than we had.

Auntie Cora offered to watch Abe and Anna so we could keep all the plates spinning. She knew we were drowning without us saying so because she *knew* us. She was parenting her own two children alone and had endured hard, lonely days. I guess she decided no one else should face those same feelings of loneliness. She only watched our children a few times per week, but I'm convinced she meticulously planned her visits. She was our very own Mary Poppins.

I would walk out of the house like a zombie-mom, trying to get my brain turned on so I could share the gospel with one of our staff in a foreign language while tackling mundane office tasks. Laundry would be piled sky high, and dirty dishes overflowed onto the counters. I'd return home a few hours later to find the laundry washed and the dishes put away. Somehow, our real-life Mary Poppins had danced through the house singing and cleaning with our then three-year-old and one-year-old in tow. The three of them would have already finished lunch, and mine would be in the microwave waiting for me. She'd smile and remind me I had to eat if I was going to feed that baby. Nap time was next. With a hug, our Mary Poppins would whisk the kids off to bed and fly to the next part of her day.

I'm not saying Auntie Cora was perfect, but for the small amount of money we paid her, the average person wouldn't have put so much love and energy into caring for our children. Having a local friend and helper in our house had major advantages. The most obvious was that she cleaned our house and took care of our children—perhaps better than we could have done ourselves. But also, having lived in Europe for a time, Auntie Cora understood our Western perspective and could explain pieces of the culture in a way that made sense.

Every missionary needs a local friend they can vent to about culture stress and frustrations. I don't mean bashing the country to a local. I mean, expressing fair frustrations to someone close. Finding a local friend who can field our complaints gives us more perspective and understanding. When a special friend explains and pushes back, it helps us assimilate and adapt.

ME. Man, it's so annoying when my favorite restaurant is out of the food I like. That happens often here.
CORA. Yeah, it is annoying. When you live in a remote area , shipping takes a while. It's tough for owners to estimate demand and keep the right amount of perishable items in stock.

Thankfully, my relationship with Cora was transparent and deep enough to withstand our cultural differences. It did not offend her when I aired a grievance. I knew I could confide in her. And she would tell me why something was the way it was. Her perspective helped me accept even the hardest parts of our new life.

Assimilating to a new culture and country is a physical and mental process. The mental transition is slower; it takes intention. That means unplugging some cords from our passport country and finding new outlets to connect to in our host country. The best way we've found to do that is to find a local friend who we connect with and who's willing to walk us through adapting to their culture.

Finding local relationships that truly encourage isn't easy. It's hard to find a friend who understands our idiosyncrasies as foreigners. It's even harder to find a friend who's lived in a country outside their own. But that's the kind of person who's most likely to understand and have compassion. God blessed us with Cora's sweet friendship about six months after moving to our city.

Empathy from a Veteran

Along with Auntie Cora, who helped us assimilate to our new home, there's a special couple we've relied on. They've shared so much wisdom with us; I can't relay it all here. Aunt Tracey and Uncle Ben are veteran missionaries. They've "been there, done that" and always have a compassionate word, a Bible verse, or a nugget of wisdom for each new situation we face. When Ron and I walk through hard days of ministry, parenting, and marriage, these two consistently affirm, encourage, and pray over us.

The year 2022 was a record low for us. Those twelve months overseas were more stressful than our first 126 months combined. In May of that year, when life was falling apart, Aunt Tracey and Uncle Ben hopped on a plane to come and help. We were suddenly in a horrible situation with our business, which led to meetings with lawyers and more tension and stress than I'd ever felt.

Aunt Tracey and Uncle Ben came and brought a few things with them. First, they brought chocolate because they are good friends. Second, they brought hearts ready to listen, pray, and encourage. Aunt Tracey and I took a walk each morning. She let me grieve and speak openly about my anger, even toward God. Uncle Ben brought calm, clear thinking for Ron as we regrouped and strategized how to move forward. And finally, they brought enough energy to love and invest in our kids. Our energy was waning. Our kids could feel our exhaustion and were expressing their own stress in their kid-like ways. Aunt Tracey read books, did puzzles, and played games. Uncle Ben attempted head stands and "cracked eggs" on the kid's heads. For a few days, we didn't have to be the ones filling our kids' cups. We exhaled. That's what happens when relief like that comes.

Four days with Aunt Tracey and Uncle Ben was enough to blow the wind back into our family's sails. The problems were still there. We still had to work through a legal situation. But we had eaten chocolate and received encouragement, and the kids were still chattering about Aunt Tracey and Uncle Ben. That was enough to keep our hands to the plow in a season when we felt like a collapse was imminent.

A support system isn't complete without a veteran missionary who's "been there, done that." The wisdom one can gain from their experience is endless. They've walked through hard days. They've been mad at God and those closest to them. They've longed to leave before God prompted them to move. And yet they've stayed in the place where God called them through their own pain and heartache. That's why they're able to coach and encourage others the way they do. They've experienced trials overseas, so they can empathize. And the best part is they are teaching us how to support others. We notice how they refresh us, and we'll do the same for new missionaries in our country.

Energy from a Volunteer
Aunt Tracey and Uncle Ben are special people who can truly empathize with a weary missionary's heart. They know how to affirm and inspire discouraged souls.

Another friend of ours, Uncle David, is an energetic volunteer who comes to visit and serve with us. Every time we host a volunteer team, like IV fluids, it infuses us with fresh energy and life! When we take volunteer teams around our city, we're reminded of the reasons we first came here. We fall back in love with our mission field. We laugh together and catch up on what's happening in our home country. Visitors renew our spirits and bring a sense of youthfulness and wonder that's rejuvenating. They're excited about the bright signs and new foods. They ask silly questions that make us laugh, like how our host country celebrates the Fourth of July. The "newness" of their thoughts and actions reminds us of our first years. That, in turn, helps to rekindle our love for this place.

Uncle David has been to our city eight times and is a joy to know. He's watched our family of two grow into a family of four. And mercy, he has experienced some of the strangest things with us! Uncle David has camped with us in ninety-degree miserable weather. He's carried giant bags of raw materials for our business around an island to be loaded onto a boat. He's helped feed our children. We've eaten bugs with him—both on purpose and by accident. The kids have tackled him, wrestling. He's washed dishes in the rain with an umbrella stuck into his shirt. And he's shared the gospel with countless souls in our state. He's a selfless guy who's a joy to host!

Of all the funny history we share with Uncle David, one story stands out the most. Ron had been talking to a local guy who said he wanted to follow Jesus. This local was...different. Danny was what we call in the US a "country bumpkin." He probably wasn't one hundred percent mentally stable. One day, we drove to his house to share the gospel with his family. Danny decided he would ride back to our house with us and stay the night. This was a matter-of-fact conversation—him telling us what would happen—not a request for permission to stay. We lived about four hours from his house, so our American brains were trying to process what this meant for the rest of our week. Where would he stay? We didn't have a spare room. Was he a safe person to have in our home overnight? How long would he stay with us? Was Danny expecting Ron to drive him back home? A lot of questions hung in the air. We tried to determine Danny's expectations but received no answers.

Ron, Uncle David, and I spoke in quiet English, making a game plan for what was about to happen. Anna was about eight months old. She slept in her crib in a separate room from us. It was our only spare room. If Danny slept in the living room, he could easily get into her room at night. Even though she was a baby, we didn't feel comfortable with that situation. We had a small bed in her room where Ron could sleep, but that would have left me by myself overnight with a stranger in the house. I wasn't comfortable with that either. Uncle David selflessly offered to come over and sleep on the living room floor with Danny, so we'd have an extra person in the house to help keep things safe. Uncle David might have slept five minutes that night. He told us our just-a-bit-kooky friend whispered alarming phrases throughout the night. That put David on high alert. He wondered if Danny was about to jump on him and chop him up with a knife.

As if the sleepover experience wasn't weird enough, the next morning was equally . . . strange. Ron left to grab a few groceries to accommodate our unexpected house guests. I stayed with our daughter Anna and Uncle David to attend to our friend. Danny used the bathroom while Ron was gone. His morning routine took about thirty minutes. We heard some weird sounds behind the bathroom door—rushing water, splashing, and noises I couldn't identify—it was bizarre. Uncle David and I sat on the couch, trying to figure out what Danny was doing. Was he showering? Making his own bidet? Washing his face? We chuckled quietly and wondered whether we should offer him a towel or just let him be. After half an hour, Danny exited the bathroom—no towel needed—in fresh clothes. Our suspicions were correct. He had showered. But how he did so is a mystery and remains so to this day.

When I opened the bathroom door, water was everywhere, flooding the floor. The ceiling was wet. The toilet was wet. The walls were wet. The sink was wet. The only area that *wasn't* wet was the shower! We do not have a hose hooked up to our toilet or a bucket for bathroom use. Yet water was dripping from the ceiling all over the bathroom. I couldn't imagine what he had done in our tiny sink to make such a mess. If he had used the shower hose, water would've been in the shower. In the aftermath, we discovered our bathroom scale had gotten so wet in the flood it ceased working. Later, we debated with Uncle David about what might have happened in the bathroom that morning. As Ron and I assimilate into the culture here, we try to understand and make sense of confusing situations like this. After a lengthy conversation, there was only one logical explanation: a hurricane had hit our bathroom—Hurricane Danny.

Going through that with Uncle David deepened our friendship. His being there and laughing with us through it injected some energy into us. When the Lord leads friends or supporters from our home country to come see us, it's one way He lifts our tired bodies up and stands us back on our feet. Uncle David has spent enough time in our city to see the cultural stress. He supports our ministry and wants to see us stay here and succeed. When we go back to the US and it feels unfamiliar, it's like a breath of fresh air to visit him. We laugh about our escapades. He asks about certain people by name. When he and other volunteers visit, they deliver living water to restore our dehydrated bodies and fatigued muscles. These volunteers are an essential part of our support system and make it easier to stay through hard seasons.

Encouragement from Afar

Introducing visitors to our life here is a gift. It fuels our ability to stay abroad, but for many, that's not feasible. Not all our supporters can fly to our ministry location to see our work firsthand. We also need encouragers who are present with us from afar.

If I made a list of my heroes of the faith, it would be a long one. I'm a pastor's daughter, so I began going to church nine months before I was born. I've met many saints who have lived godly lives in service to the Lord. Among them is my Aunt Jackie. Her life story isn't dramatic, but it's filled to the brim with hard moments of faithfulness. Like saying yes to the Lord even when it hurts. Or walking through pain while surrendering to God's will. Her quiet life of faith is quite a bright light, shining for many to see. Someday in heaven, she'll

TO STAY OR FLEE

receive many thanks from believers she encouraged along the way.

It's not surprising that my Aunt Jackie is compassionate and encouraging. She comes by it honestly. My grandma was one of the best encouragers ever. During our first year of marriage, Ron and I were both working and full-time college students. When Grandma heard we'd had a bad day, she would send a card with a sweet note and two dollars. On the card, she would write, "Take Veronica to Dairy Cream on me." Grandma didn't realize it was Dairy Queen. She also didn't recognize that two dollars wouldn't buy much ice cream, but that wasn't the point. It was her way of compassionately noticing hardship and walking beside us.

Aunt Jackie learned from Grandma, but she's the 2.0 version. Connecting with Grandma from our host country was...complicated. She needed some technical support. So I say 2.0 because Aunt Jackie is savvier about technology. Video calls, instant messaging, and email are major blessings. They keep us connected with family, friends, and co-workers worldwide.

COVID-19 shuttered our family in the house for days on end. It was an intense time. Our country was extremely strict. Most days, I could pull myself together and make it through. Other days, our extroverted family was on the verge of imploding. One day, while Ron was out distributing food and I was home with the kids, I broke down. What was the point of being overseas and locked in a house? We couldn't talk to the lost people we were trying to reach while sitting in our home. I turned to someone who I knew would encourage me. I called Aunt Jackie. To put it mildly, I vented, but it was more like a tantrum.

"I can't do this! How do I even meet with God when it's *never* quiet in this house? I'm *never alone.* I need to get out of here! My life is pointless right now!" I ugly cried as I sat slumped on the floor in our kitchen. Aunt Jackie responded in a few ways. First, she connected with me and made me feel like a normal human. She told me I wasn't crazy, even though I felt crazy. She validated my feelings and the fact that this was very hard. *I felt normal.* Second, she sat with me in the pain and allowed me to express my frustration. *I felt heard.* Finally, she shared several verses and stories with me and reminded me that God will meet me where I am. What's important is my desire to meet with Him. With that in mind, I could find refuge and the Lord's peace even while locked in my chaotic house. *I felt encouraged.*

I need people like Aunt Jackie in my life—friends who listen without trying to fix the problem or explain it away. It's human nature to act like Job's friends. We reason why a bad thing happened. We assign blame. We want to fix it. But that's not what I needed. I needed someone to sit in the bad with me—who was okay with my emotional reaction. I've learned that when a friend sits with me in hard times, it provides space for me to process. Their company, understanding, and compassion help me move out of that hard place faster. That, paired with well-timed words of encouragement, can pull me out of pitfalls.

Encouragers from afar are a vital part of staying overseas. It helps to know friends are a phone call away. And when they reach out, it's always timely. Aunt Jackie is a gifted encourager. She deserves a lot of credit for the length of time we've stayed overseas. She tells me she's proud of me and that I'm her hero, but I wouldn't have survived all the battles without her prayers, compassion, and encouragement. Uplifting conversations and messages are a reason our family remains on the field despite wanting to flee at times.

I'm so thankful for friends, family, and colleagues who help us stay overseas. Hard days happen, but the Lord doesn't want us to live through them alone. He created the global church for that reason. Believers can lessen each other's burdens through words and actions. Life is busy, but we need to be there for each other. It takes intention to maintain relationships, but it's not impossible. For many people overseas, "out of sight, out of mind" is a struggle both ways. We reap what we sow. It takes work to build and sustain a robust support system, but on hard days, it's often the thing that helps us stay and not flee.

CHAPTER 6

Invasive Questions

When Your New Culture Wounds You

Cultural Differences

Each culture reflects the Creator in a way. Maybe it's a country's hospitality—how they welcome new guests. It could be a people's ability to stand boldly in the face of fear. Or maybe it's the way they love and care for "the least of these." There's beauty in every nation. Yet, because of the fall, the opposite is also true. Sin and darkness occupy every nation.

As global citizens, we have the benefit of learning from a mix of cultures. Living abroad offers fresh ideas on how to live. We sometimes realize the error of our own ways and adopt new methods. However, living in a culture vastly different from your own also provides ample opportunity for offenses. Sometimes Ron and I are affronted by lifestyle differences we'd normally overlook, but sometimes they're situations we laugh about.

Take, for instance, the time our son lost his water bottle at a vacation resort. We were actively teaching him responsibility, so I seized the opportunity for him to practice. I instructed him to walk around the pool and lobby areas to ask the staff if they had seen or found his bottle. No one had, so we asked him to tell the front desk to contact us if they found it. I was hoping this would teach him to be responsible for his belongings and to speak up for himself.

Well, that lesson was a flop. When he asked the lead manager to let us know if they found the bottle, she replied, "You wait right here!" She came back with a fancy new resort bottle. Ron and I shook our heads and laughed. So now the lesson he's learning is when you lose something, just ask someone, and they'll give you a new one. That was a laugh-it-off kind of situation.

But other encounters are not benign cultural differences. They're an obvious result of the fall and the sinful nature of people who live in darkness. What do we do when the people we're trying to reach wound us? That's not an easy question to answer. Learning not to take it personally is a good start. Giving grace is helpful. Probably the best advice I've received is to react slowly.

Infertility

We were three months into language school when we learned that having babies wouldn't be as easy as we'd hoped. Our emotions ranged from confusion to anger to regret. Learning about infertility treatment in a foreign country where we could only form a three-word sentence was confusing. We were angry because "We moved all the way over here for *You*, God, and now here we are, unable to fulfill the first command You gave mankind—be fruitful and multiply." We regretted waiting years to try after being told it would be easier to move overseas as a family of two.

"Hopeless" isn't a word I like to throw around, but infertility elicits that desperate feeling. Every month, my body reminded me it wasn't working as it should. The lively children around me constantly took me back to the pain. It was the first time in my life I had run up against the limitations of my own power. I was not in control. At first, my meticulously planned schedule made me feel omniscient. I could say what I did and when. Then infertility. I could not say when I would become pregnant. I was in control of nothing.

Before our first trip to the infertility specialist, I searched for a doctor in our area who was female and could speak English. I wanted to talk to another girl. I needed a heart-to-heart, I-gotcha kind of conversation. We read articles and prepared ourselves, although how do you even *truly* prepare yourself for *that* talk? Would test results show we'd never be able to have children? Or would we need expensive procedures we could no longer afford? I worried we would melt down in a foreign country where we had little support. Would we end up on a plane back to the States in less than a year? My stomach was in knots as we waited for the appointment. No matter how much we prepared, infertility was not something we were ready to reckon with our first year on the mission field.

I love many things about Asia. But the way they practice medicine isn't one of them. In my home country, most doctors encourage dialogue. I appreciate that. I like asking questions and knowing details. I feel less out of control when I know what's happening around me, or in this case, *inside* of me.

Healthcare in the United States is a great fit for me. I'll bring my list of thirty-five questions. Then I'll rapid-fire them until I'm satisfied and can agree to a treatment plan. My mother is the same way. Doctors may not be excited to have patients like us, but I can't recall an

American doctor who hasn't answered my questions. Type A Veronica functions well with this type of healthcare. I try to understand the illness as much as possible. Then I surrender to treatment.

In Asia, treatment is more dictated than discussed. To ask questions in many healthcare settings is to question the doctor's intelligence, which is taken offensively. Sick stomach? Take this medicine three times a day for two weeks. Done. Will this medicine cause drowsiness? Interfere with my ability to work or sleep? Who knows? But it is the *prescribed* solution, so it *is* the solution. No questions asked. It's not like the doctor rushes me out of the office before I can ask questions. It's how a doctor reacts when I do ask something. Their firm, proud body language conjures an imaginary wall between them—the educated doctor—and me—their uneducated patient. Of course, not all doctors are this way, but many are. All that to say, asking questions in a healthcare setting here is intimidating.

I read an article once from an expat blog about this topic. They suggested sharing with each new healthcare provider how one's passport country handles medicine (for example, we like to ask questions), so the healthcare provider won't be offended. That's a smart strategy to avoid culture clashes.

Back to infertility. That first appointment with an infertility specialist was massively awkward. The procedures were not explained and were humiliating. The English-speaking doctor we had requested was less of an English speaker and more of just a doctor. We asked many questions and received few answers. Actually, we received the same few answers over and over to different questions. Here's one I won't forget.

ME. Do you think we will ever be able to get pregnant?
DOCTOR, *her English answer.* People like you like to get pregnant.

Thankfully, the answer in my brain didn't come out of my mouth. "Yes, people like me who are facing infertility *do* like to get pregnant! That was, in fact, why we scheduled the appointment and waited a month to see you! *Because we would like to get pregnant!*"

Six months later, after frequent appointments, countless tests, and plenty of cash handed over, we were no wiser. We still didn't know if we could conceive a child. Nor did we know if we could spur the process along. That alone, in the middle of learning a foreign language and pushing through our first year overseas, was tough. But even harder was conversing about the topic with locals.

For three months, I had naively introduced myself as Veronica, who was from America and had been married for seven years. I remember the first day I understood someone's reply. We were sitting in a little fried rice shop on the side of the road. It matched our budget at $0.50 per person. We had eaten at this tiny dive many times. I'm sure they knew who I was, but I introduced myself out of habit. It was the day after our first infertility appointment.

SHOP OWNER, *male.* Wow, seven years? You don't have kids yet?
ME. No, not yet. We have waited. I was in school, then Ron was in school . . .
SHOP OWNER, *a smile stretching across his face.* Oh, so you don't sleep together?

Did this man just inquire about our level of intimacy on the side of the road in a fried rice food stall? Yes. Yes, he did. I forced a polite smile and muttered something like, "No. It's not like that. This is just our culture. It's different from the culture here."

If I close my eyes, I can recall everything about that moment. The man had long hair pulled into a ponytail. Scooters beeped as they whizzed by. The smell of freshly fried rice contended with a nearby stench of foul drainage water. I had goosebumps on my arms from the cool mountain breeze. I felt my body tense up at his remark. Sorrow and grief swept in while the world swirled around me. His "joke" felt like a stab in my side, a very painful wound. I was in shock. The weight of his careless words was crushing. Why would he say that to me? Offense quickly rose in my heart.

The fact is, in this area of the world, newlyweds are encouraged to have babies right away. Ron and I married at a young age. We were still pursuing our education, so having kids right away was not a goal of ours. That's normal in the United States. That wasn't the case in our new host culture.

Invasive Questions

A second cultural difference hurt my heart even more, though. One I can't say is any easier to handle today. Americans generally steer clear of asking someone questions that might be uncomfortable to answer, especially if it's about a sensitive topic. It's an unspoken cultural rule that most follow. However, in our new bold host culture, a couple's intimacy is apparently an acceptable topic of conversation. Questions about extremely personal or sensitive topics are completely okay. So there I was, facing one of the most painful situations of my life while learning how to stomach a substantial difference in culture.

That side-of-the-road conversation led me to a long dialogue with God about infertility. For over a week, I vented. I told Him He was wrong and that infertility is stupid. But it didn't take long for me to realize this was something He wanted me to surrender to Him. Going overseas wasn't enough. He was waiting for me to surrender control of my life.

Over the course of a few weeks, the Lord softened my heart. One night as I sat with Him in our dark bedroom, I sensed Him asking me, "If your story of infertility is what I want to use to bring salvation to these people, will you allow Me to use it? You say you want to see their salvation. Are you willing to minister to these people, even from your most painful place? Even when they wound your heart?"

To be honest, those weren't questions I wanted to answer. I didn't want to tell God no, but a yes meant putting my wounded heart on display for the world to see. It felt unsafe, like jumping off a twenty-story building. I wanted to hide my pain until I had a handle on it and could distance myself from it. I didn't want to talk about my pain with strangers while I was going through it.

But God won. By the end of the night, I replied, "Lord, if this is what you want to use, I'm yours. Send me." I had no idea what that statement would bring. I just knew if I had uprooted my entire American life to be here serving the Lord, it would be counterproductive to start my new life in Asia with a big fat "NO THANKS!" to God. How hypocritical would that be? I couldn't expect success as a missionary if I started my career with a resounding no.

Rarely does a yes to God yield an immediate change in my heart, but it did that time. My heart felt lighter. Questions about our fertility continued to pop up with surprising frequency, but God gave me the strength to answer them with grace. As I acknowledged my raw place of pain to people, the Lord sent woman after woman to me who needed His love. I don't know how many women cried to me about infertility. Either their husbands no longer saw them as beautiful, their in-laws had requested a divorce, or friends were encouraging their husbands to get a second wife. There were more than I can count.

I met and prayed with woman after woman over the next three years—women who were walking through the same pain I was feeling. The difference between them and me is the Creator I serve calls me loved, valued, and beautiful amidst that agony. Although sharing my heartache about infertility felt risky, I'm so glad I did. God used it for good. Finding purpose in my pain made those years easier.

Pregnancies

While I ministered to ladies who were also facing infertility, two back-to-back blows made me cry uncle. Because infertility treatments weren't covered by our healthcare plan, we had to weigh each attempt. One month, I took a hormone supplement, which is a cheaper alternative. Aside from feeling like my head was in a vice grip all day, it was great. I say that with thick sarcasm. Not long after, I experienced a painful health issue that lasted about a week. I hadn't taken a pregnancy test yet, but it felt like a possible loss. My body and soul were weary.

Two weeks after that, we attended a wedding. The people in this area are loud and full of laughter. We thought it would give us opportunities to share the gospel and laugh. Both are healing to our souls. But on this trip, laughter eluded us. As I socialized at the wedding, two friends made a point to catch up with me individually. Both said something to the effect of, "My daughter/son married three months ago. You attended the wedding. They are expecting a baby. Why don't you have a baby yet?"

Two different ladies were talking about two different pregnancies. I'd shared the gospel with each of them at previous weddings, so it seemed as if they were questioning my God more so than my situation. Their silent insinuation wounded me again: Why would God bless them and not me? Was my God real? I imagined them challenging my faith and values. Their probing was painful and personal—the heaviest blow yet from the people I was attempting to serve.

As I endured those excruciating exchanges inside, Ron stood outside talking to a new friend. He was sharing the gospel in depth, and the man was interested in hearing more about Jesus. I held it together long enough for Ron to finish his discussion and make plans for a time to follow up. It was a win for him, but as I pulled open the door of our truck, my tears gushed. I flopped in the passenger seat, bent over, and sobbed as we escaped via the bumpy village roads. They had tested me to my limit, and I felt defeated. Again. Why do these people lack manners? Don't they see my pain? The evening was somber. I cried myself to sleep in Ron's arms.

The next morning, I woke up at rock bottom. I resolved not to try another hormone treatment. I had no interest in tracking anything. I conceded to the Lord that His will be done. If that meant I would not bear a child, I would accept it. As I sat sobbing sorrowfully, the Lord took me to a verse that calmed my heart. "You keep track of all my sorrows. You have collected all my tears in your bottle. You have recorded each one in your book" (Psalm 56:8 NLT). I remember the Lord almost audibly spoke to me, "Veronica, your earthly father has cried with you through this pain. Don't you know I care even more than him? I love you, child. I see your agony. It pains me to see you hurting." After sitting with the Lord and receiving His comfort, I was able to move forward.

A week after my woeful wedding experience, I woke up in the wee hours of the morning feeling queasy. Ron was still asleep. As I made my way to the bathroom, it hit me—this is a sign of pregnancy. I took a pregnancy test and ran back to the bedroom. "Ron! You're going to be a dad!" Ironically, I had been pregnant the prior Saturday as I journaled about the pain in my heart. I had been pregnant when I cried myself to sleep in Ron's arms the night before that. And I had been pregnant at the wedding where the women jeered at me.

I hesitate to share this story, because not everyone's story has an ending like ours. The Lord's answer to my prayers isn't a result of my goodness—just His sovereign plan. It's what He chose to do to bring glory to Himself in that place and time.

I still love on ladies who are hurting, but my conversations are markedly different. When discussing infertility before my pregnancy, I could focus the conversation on why my husband remained faithful to me and how I knew my worth—we have a biblical worldview. It was an opportunity to declare the difference in God's kingdom.

But since our happy ending, empathetic exchanges have turned into inquiries on how to get where I am. What doctor did I see? How were the procedures at the doctor's? How many months passed between infertility and pregnancy? And to think if I had told the Lord, "Wait until I'm out of this hard thing." I would have missed out on ministering to all those hurting women.

It's hard to live in a culture that pokes at heartache for fun. That's a result of the fall, not a benign difference. When barbs confront me, I'm tempted to block a painful punch with pride. "My culture is better because at least we don't do *that*." And "*I'm* better because I would never talk to *you* like that." But pride won't heal my wounds. My heart and culture are sinful, too. Taking people's sins personally is a grave mistake. I must suppress judgement and pride and extend grace and forgiveness. I don't want someone's sin to produce sin in my heart. Jesus set the ultimate example while hanging on the cross when He prayed, "Father, forgive them, for they do not know what they are doing" (Luke 23:34 NIV).

CHAPTER 7

Airplanes and Helicopters

When We Faced Fear, Trauma, and Loss

Jesus said, "Here on earth you will have many trials and sorrows. But take heart, because I have overcome the world" (John 16:33 NLT). Fortunately, no one can foresee the future. That knowledge is reserved for God alone. If I were omniscient and knew what lie ahead in my life, I would probably hide in a cave. Ron and I have encountered fear, trauma, and loss in the US on furlough and in our country of service. At times, we've felt like fragile trees in a hailstorm—bent and close to breaking under a torrent of trials. The most painful seasons have involved our children or medical emergencies.

Baby One

As if the hardship of infertility wasn't enough, my pregnancies came accompanied by their own drama. At seven months pregnant with our long-awaited first child, I noticed my body was failing to do a very basic part of pregnancy—grow. The pregnancy books told me I was supposed to look like an elephant at that point, but I was still little Veronica with a tiny baby belly. My local gynecologist assured me, "It's okay sweetie, she's still moving. That's all that matters."

However, at our seven-month appointment, we learned movement isn't *all* that matters. According to the ancient ultrasound machine there, our baby had lost weight since the last scan a month prior. My doctor sat in silence, drawing a deep, pensive breath as she thought through what to say to me. The silence was suffocating. I interjected, "What's going on?"

My doctor replied, "Well, she's smaller than she was last month."

"Is she going to be okay?!" I was on the verge of tears.

"I don't know."

There are many ways my doctor could have responded. That wasn't the reply I was hoping to hear. She explained when this happens, miscarriage becomes a concern. Along with that, blood circulation might also be an issue. She recommended we get an in-depth scan on our baby's heart and brain. A premature delivery might be necessary. Unfortunately, the technology wasn't available in our small, not-quite-first-world city. We'd have to travel elsewhere.

The tears flowed as I changed my clothes, packed my belongings, and headed to the truck. It was the same truck that carried my slumped, sobbing body over the bumpy village roads seven months prior. Now, instead of the sorrow of no life within me, my tears flowed at the possibility of a life lost within me. Ron settled our bill as I sat in the car by myself. Would we ever meet our baby girl? If we delivered, would she be okay?

We had tickets to fly to a neighboring country the next day to finalize our visas, but I couldn't go to a third-world country in my condition. After a few tearful conversations with an American doctor, we flew instead to a country that had better medical care. We made plans to meet with a gynecologist who would have an ultrasound machine manufactured after the year 2000. The visa situation was no longer our top concern.

That night, our mood was somber—much like the weekend I cried uncle over infertility wounds and then cried myself to sleep in Ron's arms after the wedding. Friends met us for pizza, but I could hardly bring myself to eat. My body felt dizzy and queasy—like at any moment, my broken heart might stop beating. "What is God doing right now?" I thought. "Why is this happening?"

Sorrow rolled in and over me like the waves of a tsunami. Did God care I was emotionally underwater, striving to save my baby from a life-threatening situation? If He was present, why would He bless us with a burst of joy for seven months, only to wipe it out with more grief?

The next afternoon, we boarded a flight knowing on the other side, we would find answers. Would this be the beginning of a miscarriage? Was my body conceding that conception was hard enough? That it couldn't carry a baby to term? We were ready for first-world medical care, but we weren't ready for what we might learn.

Due to a delayed flight, we arrived at the clinic after closing time. I was crying. It was a Friday night, but the doctor had graciously waited for us long past his time to go home. As we walked in, Ron held it together so he could tell the doctor what had happened in more detail. Then, the ultrasound. The day before, the measurement of another machine inflicted deep pain on my heart. I could hardly breathe as he squeezed the gel onto my stomach.

The doctor inspected the sonogram for what seemed like an eternity. Then he said, "She's small. But she seems to be a bit bigger than your doctor measured yesterday."

"Oh, praise the Lord!" I quickly replied.

The doctor looked at me. "Are you a Christian?"

"Yes."

"Are you missionaries?" he prodded.

Our normal reply to this question was to deflect to other topics. Missionaries weren't welcome in our host country. However, Ron quickly remarked, "Yes." My heart skipped a beat. I felt a flash of panic.

But the doctor immediately eased our anxiety. He stopped, prayed over the baby in my tummy, and promised to do whatever he could to help. Tears gushed. This time, they were tears of thanksgiving. Not thanksgiving because our baby was fine—that was still to be determined. But thanksgiving because I knew then the Lord was indeed with me. He quickly answered my question about his whereabouts by saying, "Here. I'm right here. Giving you a doctor who will pray over you as you walk through this pain."

That night, I was admitted to a hospital so staff could monitor the baby's heart rate and my vital signs every few hours. Ron wasn't allowed to stay with me. I drifted in and out of sleep between evaluations, but when I was awake, the Spirit of the Lord kept me calm. The next day would be busy with more tests. We would travel to another hospital for additional scans of our baby's brain, heart, and umbilical cord.

We were not yet in the clear, but my heart was settling into a state of worship. When I woke up the next morning, I sat alone by the hospital room window. I remember looking at flowers outside and singing.

> Great is thy faithfulness, O God my Father,
>> there is no shadow of turning with thee;
> thou changest not, thy compassions they fail not;
>> as thou has been thou forever will be.
> Great is Thy faithfulness! Great is Thy faithfulness!
>> Morning by morning new mercies I see;
> All I have needed Thy hand hath provided—
>> great is thy faithfulness, Lord, unto me![1]

Indeed, there were new mercies that morning. All we needed He was providing. His presence—that's what we needed. Our problem persisted, but the Lord was there in that place, carrying us. He was there in the uncertainty just as He had been there through infertility. Looking

---

[1]Chisholm, Thomas. "Great Is Thy Faithfulness." Hope Publishing Company. Accessed June 10, 2023. https://www.hopepublishing.com/find-hymns-hw/hw2660.aspx

back, I know He'd been with us through each painful period no matter our location. His presence doesn't guarantee our safety or a simple solution, but He promises, "I will never leave you or abandon you" (Hebrews 13:5 CSB).

In that moment, I understood the heart of Moses when he said, "If your Presence does not go with us, do not send us up from here" (Exodus 33:15 NIV). Moses had watched his people suffer under the oppression of Pharoah. He lived in exile after growing up an outsider to his own people. Moses suffered heartache. He knew hardship. After experiencing God's presence at the burning bush, he bravely told Pharoah to let His people go. He persevered through years of pain in the wilderness, leading God's people toward the Promised Land. Moses didn't know what lay ahead, but he knew he would get through it with the Lord.

I finally got it. Hard things happen, especially when the enemy feels threatened by us. Satan tempts us to turn and flee from trials. But if we persevere, God will use trials to strengthen us. The most important thing is the Lord's presence. If He's with us and we are in Him, then we're fireproof. We have *staying power.* His grace is sufficient for us, for His power is made perfect in our weakness.[2]

---

[2] 2 Corinthians 12:9

The rest of my pregnancy and the delivery were similarly traumatic. Prior to delivery, we made another trip to the emergency room. My birthing plan flew out the window. The same doctor who prayed with us when we met him prayed with us again before my C-section at thirty-eight weeks. He delivered our baby girl two weeks early because she was breech, and we were high-risk. During the surgery, they discovered the umbilical cord was wrapped around the baby's neck three times. If we had waited forty weeks to deliver, our daughter probably wouldn't have made it. Afterward, I had to stay in the ICU because of a blood clot scare. But God's presence was real. That was the scariest time of our lives, but the feeling of Him carrying us through was almost tangible. God was there. Maybe the point of it all was to see if we would stay there with Him.

Anna's arrival was intense, but we all survived. I'm so grateful for God's provision and protection through it. We became a family of three! Anna's a bundle of joy and energy. Her eyes literally sparkle when she's excited. As a baby, she would belly laugh at her dad and scream wildly when we made it to a friend's front door. Her middle name should have been Joy. We love and appreciate her exuberant spirit.

Baby Two

After waiting so long to become pregnant with our first, I imagined Anna would be an only child. Or at least there would be a sizeable gap between her and a potential sibling. Well, I was wrong. Two weeks after I stopped nursing her—surprise! I was pregnant again. We were in the United States for a five-month furlough, traveling between Ron's hometown and mine.

I have severe morning sickness when I'm pregnant. We had stopped at a hotel to spend the night. The next morning, I woke up heaving. We looked at each other with excitement, guessing what that meant. A truck stop was next door. After checking out, we thought maybe we could purchase a pregnancy test there. That would be a fabulous story for our child's baby book. I imagined telling him or her in my best redneck accent, "We found out you were a bun in the oven at a dirty truck stop on I-70." Sadly, the truck stop was out of pregnancy tests. I'm still disappointed by that. We settled for a Walgreens a few exits down. I took a test there, and it was positive!

Our plan was to head back to our host country in two months, after spending time with my family. Missionary housing wasn't available initially, so we stayed with my parents. We told them about our pregnancy right away, knowing that the next morning they would *hear* that I was pregnant.

It was fun sharing the news in person with them. Unfortunately, about six weeks later, we headed to an emergency room again. But this time, when I feared my body was trying to evict the tiny baby in my tummy, my reaction was different. I tearfully whispered to myself, "The Lord gives, and the Lord takes away. Blessed be the name of the Lord."[3] The Lord had grown my faith. Apparently, God felt that lesson (of running to Him for safety) was one we *really needed* to learn if we were to last long-term in a foreign place. Another pregnancy gave us another chance to apply what we had learned.

Obviously, my body isn't a fan of growing little people. That trip to the ER was the first of many. It brought about an unexpected one-year hiatus in the United States that had us house-hopping every few months. For the first six months of pregnancy and through several moves, I was on and off bedrest (but mainly on). And by "on bedrest," I mean the doctors told me to eat while lying down. There were many days I sat in our borrowed home, timing contractions to decide if we'd need the hospital's help to keep our bun in the oven again. I often went to the hospital for an IV treatment to slow the contractions.

At twenty weeks, we went to the hospital to tour their NICU. There was a strong possibility our baby would

---

[3] Job 1:21 CSB

come early and need extra support. I remember sobbing as Ron wheeled me through a dimly lit room. We were facing a traumatic pregnancy again. But this time, I had a false sense of safety. We were in the Motherland. It would all be fine. My family was here. Walmart was here. Good doctors were here. There would be no emergency plane ride to better healthcare. Or so I thought.

After we toured the NICU, my doctor dropped a bomb. If our baby came soon, they were not equipped to help us. I'd have to be at least twenty-eight weeks along to deliver safely there. That was eight whole weeks away. Fifty-six days. That meant my aching body would have to hold out for 1,344 more hours. If the baby came now, he would not make it. They would attempt to fly him by helicopter to a bigger city, but he'd have to go there by himself. His odds of survival would be extremely low.

Wait, what? A helicopter? No! This is America. We don't need planes and helicopters. We have perfectly good hospitals on every street corner, right? I had a flash-back to my first pregnancy—us flying to another country for a detailed ultrasound, then deciding which country to have Anna in. But this was *America*. Abe would be born *here*. America is our Motherland—the place where we are safe. Our job isn't a secret here. Walmart is just down the road. And babies can be born without drama.

God was poking at my false sense of security. I realized whether I was in my host country or home country, His presence was my safety, not a modern hospital. A false sense of security misled my heart, promising assurances only God Himself could provide. God alone is omnipotent.

As a missionary, I associate my home country with feelings of safety and "better" goods and services. If we were having this baby in America, it would be drama-free because the doctors are better there. If I were in the Motherland, I could get pasta without bugs in it. If we lived in America, our kids' classmates wouldn't bully them for being different. Had America become a god to me? Ouch. Yes. It had.

Apparently, the Psalmist didn't say, "Those who live in the shelter of America will safely deliver their babies." My pregnancy with Abe was scary. I was on bedrest for twelve weeks. We went to the hospital multiple times so I could get an IV to slow my contractions. Days were lonely and long in a borrowed home by myself.

A few days before Abe's delivery, I met with my OB-GYN. I was exactly thirty-six weeks and three days pregnant. She congratulated me on keeping the baby in my stomach as long as I had and jokingly said, "Ok, you keep him in there four more days so he can be a full-term baby." I guess I'm good at following directions because I went into labor exactly four days later.

Throughout this intense pregnancy, another issue loomed. My family has a history of a bleeding disorder. It only manifests in males. My mom was a carrier, but we didn't know if I was. Because of the bedrest order, I couldn't receive the gene testing to see if I was a carrier. When Abe was born, his toes and fingers were blue. This would be mildly concerning for a "normal" baby, but because of my family history, the operating room turned into chaos. Specialists whisked him off this way and that.

I finally held my little guy about two hours after he was born. Our organization informed us we would have to move to a less remote location if Abe did indeed have the bleeding disease. It would be too risky to live in our city. Of course, his health was our primary concern, but this added anxiety about whether another big life change was on the horizon. Doctors told us the treatment would be intense. Any major bumps, bruises, or cuts could turn life-threatening and would require an immediate trip to the ER. Thankfully, at three months old, doctors ruled Abe would not be a bleeder.

Today, Abe is a ball of bouncy energy. If we had a way to harness his pep, it would power our entire house. I don't have a brother, but I hear this is typical of little boys. He's also compassionate, leaving sweet cards in special places for his family to find. He firmly believes Jesus is the Way to salvation, and he wants to follow Jesus alone. I'm so grateful for Abe. I'm also thankful our little bouncy ball does not have a bleeding disorder. We'd need a frequent flyer card for the ER or bubble wrap if he did!

Two traumatic pregnancies—one in Asia and one in America. Both taught me to trust my Father for safety. God was telling me, "Veronica, no place on earth will satisfy your need for comfort. True peace is only attained in My presence."

I think He was preparing us for what was to come—a cancer scare, near-death experiences, pain, and betrayal. If we trusted this one lesson—running to His presence for safety—nothing the enemy threw at us could make us flee the field.

What have I learned when fear, trauma, and loss incessantly beat on us? I have learned to cling to my King. We have a King who can sympathize with our weaknesses. He understands my pain. Some days I take longer to return to my place of safety in Him, but that's where I find comfort. I try to move and rest in the shelter of the Most High. The Lord taught me how to do that through the stress and uncertainty of my pregnancies.

CHAPTER 8

Change

When Seasons of Life Shift

Change—it's inevitable. Sometimes we initiate changes ourselves. Like that one time, I thought it would be fun to dye my hair pink. Not to say that was a wise decision, but I was in control of the situation. Chinese New Year may not be the time to go pink, though. "Gong xi fa cai!" (Wishing you prosperity in the coming year) said every single person as they walked by me. The city flowed with colors of red and pink to celebrate the holiday. So did my hair. But there are other changes we have little to no control over—like adjusting to a new season of life.

A New Schedule

Prior to Anna coming into the world, Ron and I had a schedule. Friday night was Small Group. That started around nine. A couple of nights a week, Ron played futsal (soccer on a smaller court) at eight while I shared stories with a friend at the mall. Church was on Sundays from ten in the morning until twelve-thirty or one. We spent the rest of the week walking the hot streets or crowded malls to engage people in gospel conversations.

It turns out our entire routine was incompatible with young children. Little humans need a good amount of sleep to be happy. While naps on the fly can happen, not every child (or mom) is cut out for them. Anna was the happiest baby. Even now, as an eight-year-old, she has a way of turning hard things into happy things. Anna was also a very snotty child. Not snotty as in conceited, but snotty as in she had a nasal issue. Congestion kept her up at night and woke her up during naps. We were all exhausted and grouchy.

As a new mom, I felt like an idiot when we finally figured out the problem. She was lactose-intolerant. The first three months of her life, she screamed almost every day, starting around 4:30 p.m. until well into the night. It was so bad that Ron would take her on walks at midnight so I could sleep. Our apartment was tiny, so there was no escaping it.

Prior to her diagnosis, we tried every suggestion in the book. People would say, "Oh it's witching hour." I thought, *"Really?* So now we're bringing witches into the equation? I'm so confused by what witches have to do with babies." We gave her gripe water. We tried letting her cry it out. But nothing worked.

Finally, we discovered she couldn't have dairy. That meant I couldn't have dairy (including dairy powder in bread) because, on top of being lactose-intolerant, she couldn't take a bottle. She choked every time we tried to give her one. Because she couldn't take a bottle, I could hardly leave the house. As much as I loved her and was so incredibly thankful for her, this massive change in my lifestyle was a shock. I knew a baby would transform our lives, but I didn't expect to be under house arrest. How would I reach the people I was living among if I could hardly leave the house?

When Anna arrived, we were three years into our life overseas. We felt settled. We had a routine. We had friends. We had responsibilities. When our new family member rearranged our schedule overnight, suddenly, we couldn't do anything we used to. Most of our ministry involved late-night get-togethers or hours out of the house. That was near impossible for me now. We were so happy to be parents, but making time for ministering was now really hard. It was defeating—being infrequent.

We were making zero impact, we reasoned. Should we really stay?

We knew in our hearts the Lord wasn't calling us to leave. But hard circumstances were tempting us. We could be close to family and have more help, I thought wishfully. Walmart probably has bottles that would work for Anna, I imagined. But I couldn't justify it. God wasn't calling us back to America.

Here's the thing. There's a difference between staying somewhere physically and staying because you're all in for God. I mean, I could say, "Sure. I guess I'll live here, God," while my heart is far away. Technically, I'd be doing what He said, but would I be truly obeying His call? There's more to staying in God's will than being physically present. The posture of our hearts is important. Serving is sometimes settling where the cloud of the Lord has led us, even though we'd rather return to Egypt. It's a decision to truly settle and be present with the people He brings to us (including our kids). There are seasons of limited productivity when children are born or health problems arise. But that doesn't mean we pack our bags.

Stuck at Home
So I told God, "Okay. We know You want us to stay here. How do I do this now as a mom? Everything has changed. I'm not making an impact. What now? Bring me people

to love, Lord, even while I'm stuck at home." And God did just that.

Due to Anna's dairy allergy and her aversion to bottles and solids, the first eleven months with her were exhausting. When we first moved overseas, I thought house helpers, nannies, and drivers were unnecessary luxuries. It was judgmental of me, I admit. Now that I'm a mom that's lived in this country for ten years, I get it. Grocery shopping takes a full day. Meals are cooked from scratch. Every. Single. Meal. Dishwashers do not exist here. And we have no family around to help. I conceded it's okay to have help. Sometimes, it's worth it to pay people to be part of our support system. The challenge here is finding a reliable, trustworthy person to help our family.

As I entered the world of dairy-free eating and cooking, I realized I desperately needed help. We had no idea how to search for a house helper, but we started asking around. Shortly into our hunt, a couple from our church said, "We have a lady who cleans our house, but she doesn't share our faith. Are you okay with that?" My heart leapt with joy! After contacting her, it was obvious she was part of the people group we were aiming to reach. I had reasoned with the Lord that I couldn't make an impact from my home. God proved me wrong and sent a lost person from our people group to my door. That's when Auntie Sarah came into our lives.

Auntie Sarah worked for us once a week. She washed the sheets, vacuumed, and mopped. She even helped cook one dairy-free meal per week. And while she worked, I chatted with her. During my honeymoon phase with Auntie Sarah, I'd sit in a chair just outside our tiny kitchen (which was about five by eight feet), and as Sarah washed dishes, I'd share stories from the Bible. I'd ask her to help me with any errors in my pronunciation or vocabulary.

Auntie Sarah was from a certain people group in our state known for being gregarious and direct. These are the people who dance with snakes and who jeered at my infertility. On one hand, their boisterous culture makes me feel right at home. On the other hand, I do not appreciate their direct comments about my personal life.

Sarah was a loud, cheerful person and an open book. She shared about every thought she had with me. Our rapid-fire exchanges went something like this:

SARAH. Misses, the baby is tired.
ME. She just woke up. I think she's rubbing her eyes because she's still waking up.

SARAH. Misses, you're too skinny. You don't look healthy.
ME. Yes, that's because I can't eat dairy. I hope it gets better.

SARAH. Misses, these vegetables you bought are way too expensive. Where did you buy them?

Sarah worked for us for six years. She made my "favorite" inappropriate comment one day after I put Anna down for a nap. I had read books, sang, and played with Anna for an hour before naptime.

SARAH, *after two minutes of Anna sleepy-grunting*. Misses, the baby is crying.
ME. She's just grunting until she falls asleep. She does this every day.
ANNA, *falls asleep within a few minutes*.
SARAH. Well, I guess she realized no one cared about her and just fell asleep.

Sarah's comments often hit a nerve. Nevertheless, I treasured opportunities to share stories from Scripture with her. Having a clean house was wonderful. But it was hard to share my space. Change. After being overseas for three years, it was no longer our norm. Change was no longer exciting and adventurous. It was annoying.

Motherly Instincts
Mothering overseas in the beginning wasn't easy. Our baby girl captivated me and blessed my heart, but I didn't

know how to be a missionary anymore. What was my calling? Taking care of Anna and the house was about all I could manage. I came overseas to serve these people, not to watch my husband do it alone. We wanted to serve together. How could I do that now? It felt impossible.

It took months to find a new rhythm. We worked hard to find windows of time when I could go share or we could get out as a family. Having a baby was helpful when it came to starting a conversation with strangers, but it was also distracting trying to keep people focused on a story from Scripture. Anna giggled and engaged everyone she met. It was a whole new ball game.

As missionary parents, the most challenging part was deciding what boundaries to place around our child in her interactions with people around us. Strangers kissed her on the face in hospital elevators. Older kids at the playground pinched her cheeks playfully until they were red. Restaurant staff stood her on top of tables and gave her an endless buffet of bananas right before dinner— fresh, fried, whatever she wanted.

Life in Asia with a little American baby was funny. We had a built-in babysitter at every meal. Was she hungry, tired, or fussy? No worries. A waitress would be over soon enough to attend to her needs. Anna would be whisked away from the table with a sweet little auntie who would talk to her, feed her, and giggle with her. Anna ate up every minute. She's never met a stranger. At our friends' houses, they carried her from room to room, presenting her like a trophy to visiting neighbors. We smiled and used the attention to share stories about the gospel.

But then came the day that was too much. We went to a loud, hot wedding with Auntie Sarah. Music blared as we approached the canopy. Sarah insisted on making an entrance by carrying Anna. She was the special auntie of this foreign baby, and she wanted the world to know. Inside, close to three hundred people crowded in a two hundred square foot space. Auntie Sarah instructed us to find a seat as she carried our baby around, showing off her prized family member. After all, we were her family by that point.

But what happened next was a nightmare situation for me as a new mom. People were passing Anna around like a hot potato. She bounced from one person to the next, each snapping a photo and pinching her cheeks. These people were strangers to me, so it was very unsettling. No one regarded me as her mother. Lips were landing on her face—maybe even her mouth—ugh!

As we sat watching in horror, I felt helpless. How could I politely say, "Give me back my baby!" I didn't know this would happen, so I had not asked local friends for advice in advance. No one trained us for this type of situation. And Anna was no help as she happily flopped from stranger to stranger.

After a few rounds, Ron retrieved Anna, saying with a big smile that it was time for her to eat. She needed her mom for that, we reasoned. But in truth, she didn't need her mother at that moment. Her mom needed her. Crashing a wedding with a baby was completely different. We didn't have the skills for this.

For days after that wedding, I felt like a complete failure. How could I let people pass my child around a pop-up tent like that? We were right off a highway. Anyone could have taken off with her. My fear of offending people paralyzed my protective motherly instincts. I was furious with myself for allowing her to be an object of interest—an attraction. I didn't want another stranger to interact with her again. I felt guilty for allowing our lifestyle to impact her like that.

Questions tumbled through my mind. Was I wrong to feel terrified when strangers held my baby and passed her around a crowded tent? Was part of my job to trust these people with my baby for the sake of the gospel? Surely, I didn't have to sacrifice her well-being for the sake of my work, did I?

Over time, the Lord taught me two things. First, when change occurs, sacrifice will follow. If I'd kept my baby from interacting with locals after that horrible situation,

I'd have stood in the way of God using Anna for His glory. God gave me a daughter, but she isn't really mine—she's His. Considering that, I concluded it was okay for strangers to hold her sometimes. Part of being a missionary is making sacrifices—in my life and in our kids' lives—for the sake of the gospel. No, they didn't choose to be missionary kids. But their parents are called to be missionaries along with caring for them. God taught me early on that my daughter would be impacted—sometimes negatively, sometimes positively—because of our profession and the culture in which we live. I can't protect my kids from every discomfort.

However, the second thing the Lord taught me in the anguish of my failure was to never put the people I serve above my family. If I'm uncomfortable with a situation and my gut tells me something is wrong, I don't have to concede for the sake of assimilation or for fear of offending. These peoples' salvation does not hang on my ability to be exactly like them or accept everything they throw my way. Should I try to adapt to and accept this new culture? Absolutely. Should I ignore my motherly instincts to win them for Christ? No. God taught me it's necessary to have boundaries. Jesus did. If Jesus could hide away and pray while people were chasing him down, demanding miracles, then it's okay for me to escape the culture stress when my heart tells me I've hit my limit.

Settled

After about five years of living here, I relaxed a little. The first five years were adventurous. Abnormal was our new normal. We didn't know what to expect. And then, over time, this area became familiar. It became our home. We put down roots without realizing it. One day we were speaking in choppy sentences to the grocery store clerk, "I . . . have . . . change . . . please?" The next, we were carrying on a detailed conversation with our waitress, forgetting we were foreigners because the city no longer felt foreign to us. Like birds who migrate south, we'd embraced the heat and culture. Had this place become home?

In this transition, something happened. As I became more familiar with my surroundings, I became less flexible regarding my routine. I recall the early days when I would open the door to our village house to find the vivacious, active bodies of twenty little kids from our village. Twenty little kids who showed up without a scheduled time to meet. Kids who were eagerly anticipating draining every last braincell from my brain. Those days were gone. Now, an unannounced visitor produced a sense of annoyance in my heart. This wasn't in our schedule for the day. We were settled.

When missionaries reach this level of settled, a few things happen. First, it becomes easier to stay than to

TO STAY OR FLEE

leave. I don't mean staying in God's will. It's always hard to stay in God's will because that's not something we do haphazardly. That takes intention, prayer, and introspection. I mean physically staying somewhere. Once we get comfortable, it's hard to leave. Our house, our car, and our life are here. We know people now, and people know us.

If we're not careful, we can easily stay in a place long after the cloud of the Lord has moved. No one wins an award for staying on the field after the Lord has told them to move. There's no glory in digging into a place when the Lord says it's time to go. But many missionaries stay overseas long after the Lord has prodded them to leave. Why? Maybe part of it is pride. For some reason, we've made staying in a location the holy grail—as if we'll win a trophy.

Other times, I think it amounts to change. Where would we go, and what on earth would we do? Over the years, this foreign place had become our home, and our home country had become foreign. When change knocked at our door, we were unwilling to entertain the idea. Instead of saying, "Here am I. Send me!"[4] we're like a disgruntled church member who's unhappy about a drum set being put onstage in the sanctuary.

---

[4] Isaiah 6:8 NIV

There's something about change that makes me cling tightly to my heavenly Father. Perhaps that's the point. Change isn't easy. It knocks me off balance. I can't function as I did before. But in that off-balance moment, I'm forced to reevaluate where I'm at. Is this change a sign the Lord is telling me it's time to go somewhere? Is He prompting me to do something or preparing my heart for a bigger change? Is He calling me to come back to Him? In response, I reevaluate my schedule, my ministry, and my family life. What adjustments do I need to make? Am I serving where I am out of habit or because of His calling that has me staying there?

Unexpected Turbulence

When Something Out of the Blue Throws Us Off Course

Change Versus Turbulence

Turbulence. I hate it. I know, I know. Planes are a constant part of my life. Most people assume since we fly all the time, we must love it. I love the part when we arrive at our destination. I hate not knowing the person in control of getting us there. I wouldn't want to fly the plane myself. Obviously, that would end in a plane crash. I'm just not a fan of someone else having the power to keep me alive or kill me. Sadly, multiple planes have fallen from neighboring skies over the last ten years. Enough to make me nervous. Each flight, I tell myself, "Airplane travel is safer than car travel." I also tell myself, "If God wants me to stay alive today, then I will. If He wants to see me at His gate today, He will. That doesn't depend on a pilot's ability." And while that helps to bring peace, flying still isn't something I *enjoy*.

We've also been through turbulent times. Turbulence is different from change in that it's unexpected. We often see change coming. Change is long-lasting and requires a shift in lifestyle. When I had a baby, my life changed. I had to learn how to adapt to life as a mom. There are unexpected changes like deaths, but something like that impacts a person for the foreseeable future. There is an adjustment period—a shift.

But turbulence is different. Turbulence hits when you were clipping along just fine. Suddenly, wham! There's a sudden interruption. It won't last. Give it a couple of weeks, a few months, or maybe a year or two. This interruption will eventually go away, but it comes out of nowhere and disrupts life. We can't move forward fully. We're stuck temporarily, yet it's simply a season. The challenge is finding a way through the situation to get back to normal life. Turbulence is weird because it arrives unexpectedly, and its end is unpredictable. In my opinion, it can wreak more havoc on overseas life than change does because of all the unknowns. An example could be an older MK who isn't adjusting well to college life in the States. Do missionary parents take a leave to go visit and support him? Will the student be able to adapt or pivot within a few months' time? Will his parents return to their overseas home? Turbulence wreaks havoc in planning.

A Business Deal Gone Bad

Some of our most turbulent months occurred a few years into opening a business overseas. Our business was based in the country where we served, but the materials we needed to source for our business were in a different country. I was nervous about raw material sourcing. Horror stories are abundant in the expat world about entrepreneurs sending a deposit for supplies and not receiving them. In my mind, foreign suppliers were a mafia we'd have to "get in" with in order to get what we were paying for. Amazon has no reviews for shady middlemen in Asia. We were on our own trying to figure this out. We had to find honest brokers who could help us make purchases. They were in the mafia too. We all but had to cut off a limb and send it to someone in the mail to prove we were serious buyers. The brokers didn't trust us either. They had probably been burned by foreigners too.

So we cautiously danced with them. We tried to do due diligence without overdoing it. If we didn't ask enough questions, we might send several thousand USD without enough vetting to be confident we'd get our supplies. If we asked too many questions—BAM—the mafia might expel us. Or if we couldn't answer their questions about the specifications of what we were ordering correctly, they would become suspicious and back out. The thing is, we didn't go overseas to start a business, so we were unsure about the specifications of the items we were sourcing. Their detailed questions on weights and compositions had us Googling our way into what we hoped would be enough knowledge to pass their test.

Eventually, we dove in and placed an order with a broker. It went surprisingly smoothly, considering it was our first purchase. The order arrived a few months late, but we received it, and the quality was fabulous. It was a win, considering a few months late in Asia is on time. Our broker's excuse for his tardiness was that he had syphilis. Maybe the delay was because of his sickness, or maybe his business just ran on "Asian Time." I personally wouldn't use syphilis as an excuse for running late.

The price had been outrageous on this first order, but otherwise, it was successful. Based on a bit of digging, we believed the price was so high because of our middleman. Thinking we were now on the inside of this Asian mafia, we decided the second time around we'd buy an even larger amount directly from the factory. Who needed a random middleman doing a quality check? We had this figured out. We'd be fine. And we'd save money.

Our second order started out okay. We'd found the location of the factories that produced the raw materials we needed. That was step one. After a few months of digging, we contacted a mom-and-pop factory that said they could be our supplier. We sent specifications—this time, much more aware of what we needed. Then we sent a deposit and confidently awaited our order.

There's a proverb based on the Bible that goes, "Pride goes before a fall."[5] Well, fall we did. Two months after paying this factory several thousand dollars, we still had nothing to show for it. We sent messages and emails and called. Every reply was, "Yes, it will be ready next week." After two months of hearing "next week," we decided "next week" could be 2076 if we didn't do something. We felt horrible. Our inexperience was leading to the loss of a very large amount of money. A very large amount of money that came from our supporters, not us. So, we did what we always do—we got scrappy. We wouldn't take no for an answer. We had hit some turbulence, but we would get through this. I warned our contact at the factory, "If

---

[5] Proverbs 16:18

the supplies are not on the way by 'next week' as you say, Ron will fly over the following week to speak with you about our order."

Maybe this hot mess of a factory had heard threats like this before, but I was positive they hadn't encountered our passion and determination. If this was their normal mode of operation, I imagined they were used to being yelled at and threatened in heated situations, but we were different. We wouldn't be yelling at them. Ron would just show up at the factory every day until they got annoyed enough to fulfill our order. "The squeaky wheel gets the grease." That's an American proverb.

To no one's surprise, the order was not ready the following week, so Ron flew to this other country to follow up. For two weeks, every single day, he went to the factory. He asked for the items we had purchased. They said, "Tomorrow, they'll be here." And then tomorrow would come, and they would say tomorrow again. This went on long enough that our supervisors told us Ron should come home. We needed to be back together as a family. But to us, Ron coming home was giving up. That would mean losing several thousand dollars that weren't ours to begin with. We were determined not to let that happen. So, we devised another plan. What if I flew with the kids to join Ron? Then, together, we would ask for our money back and find a new factory. Our supervisors okayed this plan.

It would be my first time flying with the kids on my own, but I was excited. We would persistently but lovingly fight for justice. The night before our trip, Asia hit me with a nasty stomach bug. Nasty as in, I could hardly walk after expelling every bit of food from my body. I needed to take my two- and four-year-old children on two flights by myself the next day, but I didn't know if I was capable. Fabulous.

The next morning, some sweet friends helped us get to the airport. We made it onto the first flight and to the next country without too many problems. Exhausted, I hauled the children through immigration, to a restaurant for lunch, and to our gate for the second flight. As we waited to board, my body was terrifyingly close to giving out. I was about twenty-four hours into fasting and running on fumes, hoping to avoid an airplane bathroom mishap. I gave myself a pep talk. "Veronica, all you need to do is get yourself and your two children onto that second plane. Ron and a hotel bed are on the other side. You can do this!"

We boarded the plane shortly after. I mustered the last of my energy and took both kids to the airplane bathroom so we could all have a nice nap on the flight. We crammed into the one-inch by one-inch bathroom (or at least that's what it felt like). I pulled Abe's pants down and discovered a disaster. My two-year-old potty-training son had needed a potty earlier, but I was unaware. Maybe he sensed I wasn't feeling well and didn't want to bother me; I'm not sure. But because I was oblivious when I pulled his pants down, the contents of said pants were now smeared all over his legs and falling onto the toilet, his shoes, the floor, and everywhere directly under him. I looked on in horror, realizing that me, myself, and I needed to clean up this mess. And I had to clean it up fast, or we would hold up an entire plane of people. My mom brain turned on. Anna would need to dash up the aisle to retrieve the diaper bag with freshly stocked wet wipes. I couldn't leave Abe standing naked with poop everywhere in the plane bathroom alone. And I couldn't clean up a mess this big without wet wipes.

Poor Anna waded up the crowded aisle to the middle of the plane as I stood at the door of the bathroom. Her two-foot-tall stature was not commanding enough to capture the attention of people who were in her way. "Excuse me!" her cute little voice squeaked. No one listened. "Excuse me!" I yelled from the back of the plane. Still, no one listened. My poor girl was stuck, unable to walk against the flow of traffic. After several minutes of her glancing back at me helplessly and then turning bravely to the crowd of people in front of her, a flight attendant noticed her. He escorted her to our seat to retrieve the wet wipes. By this point, other attendants realized this mom was all on her own with an *enormous* mess.

When Anna returned with wet wipes and a trash bag gifted by the flight attendant, I frantically began wiping up the mess. Now with hardly enough energy to stand and in a horrible mood, I lectured Abe harshly. "Why didn't you tell Mommy you needed to go poop? You know you go poop in the toilet, not in your pants." Anna interjected, "But Mom, you have to be patient with him. He's still little." I thanked Anna for the reminder (maybe a bit sarcastically) and finished scrubbing the now caked-on residue off Abe's legs. I cleaned up the mess, and then we made it back to our seats without delaying the flight. And despite feeling self-conscious about having poop on me (which didn't help my squeamish stomach), we were all able to relax and take a nap before reaching Ron on the other side.

A Showdown with the Boss

Once I had a day or two to recover, we went to the factory and returned daily. Then the workers' fasting month began. So now, not only were they not giving us our order for who knows what reason, but they were also grouchy and unwilling to meet us because they were tired. We endured a week of hauling our children to and from the factory, trying to find the person in charge who could help us. When we finally did, we firmly told him we wanted our money back since they had not fulfilled our order. He looked at us apathetically, like, "Who cares?" But we bugged him until he gave us the location of their office and arranged a meeting with his boss.

The next afternoon this same man welcomed us, well maybe less welcomed and more let us into, the office of this factory. The office was the size of a small bedroom, maybe eight by ten feet. There was no air conditioning or fan. Samples of all sorts were stacked here, there, and everywhere, making the actual floor space about four by five feet. The manager we had been working with motioned for us to sit on the floor. So there we were in a tiny, hot office, sitting on a dirty floor with our two small children. We figured if the kids got fussy, it would only benefit us. We waited for the boss to arrive.

Fifteen minutes later, the boss walked in. He was tall and thin with tired-looking eyes. We demanded that he return our money. I said, "Ron has been waiting three weeks for you to hand over our order. It hasn't come. We'll find a different factory, but we need our money back. Either give us our money back or give us the raw materials we've ordered, and we'll bill you for the flights, hotel, and food expenses we've incurred over the last three weeks. Here's the list showing what this trip has cost us." I handed him the paper. Ron and I had jotted down our expenses and decided we'd be happy if they gave us fifty percent of what we requested. We'd negotiate. Considering we were dealing with the mafia, if we recouped some of our money and lived to tell about it, that would be a win.

The lanky boss replied, as if he was on the verge of dying, "I'm fasting right now. I'm tired. Let's meet later after I break fast; then we can talk."

Anger stirred in my heart as I thought, "Listen, mister, I cleaned up a toddler poo-nami on an airplane by myself hours after I barfed my guts out because of you. You are not dying. You are fasting."

I quickly replied, "You have said 'next week, tomorrow, and later' after every single inquiry we've made. We're tired of hearing 'later.' We will sit right here on this floor until you bring us our money." We had heard so many excuses over the last three months. Now religion was the latest excuse. I was over it.

The boss replied, "But you don't understand. I'm hungry and tired. I've not eaten since breakfast. Just wait until tonight. We'll meet again and give you your money, then."

"I don't care what you do, but our family isn't leaving this floor until we have our money back." His religious excuse for being horrible to work with had hit a nerve.

The boss replied defensively, "I know, but we're fast-ing. We haven't eaten since breakfast. I can't think straight because I haven't had food. It's not easy. We can meet you after we break fast."

At that, my filter fell, and what was in my head came out before I thought it through. "In my religion, we fast too. But we're told not to act gloomy but to wash our hair and face. We shouldn't make it obvious that we're fasting because we're not fasting for others to see, but for God to see. We get up, do our work, and don't tell anyone about our fasting because it's for God alone." Ron chipped in, "I don't know. Maybe your fasting is different."

The boss quickly stood and left the room, obviously of-fended by my statement. The manager was still in the room with us. Feeling the tension, I awkwardly shared more with the manager about our fasting, trying to smooth over my outburst. Minutes later, the boss re-turned and gave us an envelope of cash equaling a full refund. We took it and sheepishly left the office, unsure of whether to count this as a win or a loss.

Oh, the Places You'll Pee!
We *had* accomplished what we came for. At least we didn't have to feel guilty about losing money that wasn't ours. Ron had also identified two new factories in the area that seemed reliable. I met with staff from both

factories to discuss future orders. That evening, we felt a celebratory dinner was warranted. We searched for the most Western restaurant in town. After arriving at the cozy café, we chose a table in a quiet corner. Relief. We had made it through a bumpy ride. It was finally over. Ron and I laughed at the ridiculous situation, embarrassed at how we got our money back, but also proud that we had. We surmised this gave us mafia boss status.

As we laughed, Anna interjected, "Mommy, I need to go potty." The waitress walked us outside and pointed at the door of the bathroom. We walked to the door and opened it. Inside the bathroom was a spigot, a sink, and two buckets. One bucket was upside down; the other was right side up. Western toilet? No. Squatty potty? Also no. Drainage hole to pee into? (Yes, we've had that experience.) "Guess I need to check for a drain," I reasoned. I lifted the upside-down bucket, expecting to find a drainage hole to pee into. To my dismay, there was no drain. The entire floor of this bathroom was cement. I held the bucket in my hand, confused. There was no Western toilet, no squatty potty, and no hole in the ground, but the waitress clearly knew what I was looking for and directed me to this place. Then it hit me. The bucket I was holding was likely a type of chamber pot. I was holding the toilet in my hand! Ew! I did what any reasonable person would do. I set the bucket down, bathed in hand sanitizer, and had a quick heart-to-heart with Anna.

"Anna, I think that bucket that mommy was just holding is the thing you're supposed to pee into." Her big brown eyes widened. I continued, "We are not going to pee into it. That is very weird—I mean different. We're going to go back to the table and quietly tell Daddy what happened. Then we'll ask him to find us a different toilet ASAP." Anna's shocked face smoothed into a slight grin. "And even though this is very strange to us and very funny, we're going to act normal when we go back to the table and wait to laugh about this weird situation until we get to the car. Can you do that?" Her grin was now a wide smile. "Of course, Mommy."

We returned to the table and shared our bathroom situation with Ron. He called over the waitress and politely asked, "Is that your toilet? Because there's no toilet." The waitress replied, "Oh, does she need to go poop?" Ron hesitated, "I'm not sure. She's four." The waitress promptly took Ron to a nice, clean bathroom in the back of the restaurant, complete with a Western toilet.

I've thought at times the title of this book should be *Oh, the Places You'll Pee!* because it seems like most of our crazy experiences overseas have had some connection to a toilet. If I had a picture of every throne we've used, I could make a very interesting coffee table book. There have been big ones, small ones, pipe-hole ones, white ones, gold ones, and middle-of-the-rice-field ones. But out of all of them, this bucket might win the medal for Most Peculiar Toilet we've seen overseas.

Looking for a Positive

Turbulence. That whole trip was unplanned. When would it end? What would happen along the way? We didn't know. We weren't expecting to travel to another country that month, let alone experience the toilet trauma and stage a small sit-in protest. This would not be our new normal. It was a period we had to maneuver through. Turbulence. There's really no way to prepare for it. It's not like our trainers said, "Now someday, if you are in the middle of a business deal with the Mafia and are getting ripped off, the godliest way to handle it is. . ." If they had, I would have probably chosen a different position at the missionary job fair. And no one could really coach us through it, either. It was just something that popped up unexpectedly and went away in time.

How should we face turbulence? Look for a positive. I didn't expect my first flight with the kids to begin with barfing and end with a poo-nami. However, I made it through on my own. I knew I'd probably have to fly alone with the kids again in the days ahead. Now that I'd done it once, future flights would be easier. To flip the negatives into a positive, I'm thankful God gave me the energy to get through that long day.

The benefit of turbulence is growth in awareness and knowledge. A challenging experience is an opportunity to learn something new—develop street smarts. We had to react according to our gut instincts. As a result, we learned about our capabilities; we learned more about the culture; and we learned how to push through that seemingly insurmountable situation. Each hardship we walk through can add to our skill set, making us more capable of tackling the next hard thing. But we miss the opportunity to grow and gain insight if we remain angry about the hard thing happening in the first place.

CHAPTER 10

Sucker-Punched

When Everyone Leaves or Disappoints You

Pre-pandemic Utopia

This wonderful city of ours once hosted a big group of missionaries. So big, in fact, that no one had a house large enough for all of us to gather. Compared to the state of things now, it was like a utopia. I took it for granted. My children had friends who were foreign like them, and I always had an empathetic ear who could relate to my plights. A month did not go by without someone inviting us to their house for a delicious Western meal they had graciously spent a few days preparing. It was a happy time in our life overseas.

Along with our fellow foreign friends, a group of locals had worked with us "crazy Americans" for so long, they understood our quirks. Local friends who can bridge the cultural gap between us are special. We were downright spoiled when we landed in this city. But then all of that changed.

Auntie Cora

The first blow to our pre-pandemic support system was the exit of our very own Mary Poppins. Auntie Cora had lived in hiding for many years because of her conversion, hoping the authorities wouldn't find out about her identity. She fielded questions from her children's school. Coworkers pried about her identity at work. And neighbors constantly asked about her background in conversation. After years of living like this, she was ready to relax. She dreamed of seeking asylum.

In 2019, our family was scheduled to return to the United States for furlough. Auntie Cora made her heartbreaking announcement before our departure. She was moving to America. Her move would fall during our time in the US, but she would be so far away, it would be nearly impossible to see her. After our time in the US, our beloved Mary Poppins would no longer be there to welcome us home. Nor could she return because of her immigration status.

I remember the day of her announcement like it was yesterday. She shared her news with excitement and a bit of apprehension. My face warmed into a smile. I told her I was happy for her. I truly was happy for her. We hugged, and she left.

As I closed the heavy, gray door of our apartment, a surge of sadness ran through my body. What would I do without Auntie Cora? She had been a constant presence in our overseas life. I walked into the kitchen in a daze and shut the door so the kids couldn't see me. I leaned against a cabinet door as tears flowed, then slid to the ground. Auntie Cora had prepared me for this day. It wasn't a surprise. But the sadness was intense. It felt like a tornado was spiraling inside of me.

Auntie Cora was part of our family overseas. We celebrated holidays with her. We laughed and cried with her through the ups and downs of life. She loved our kids as if they were her own. She was like a sister to me and an aunt to our kids. This was their first big TCK goodbye. The announcement of her departure felt the same as our departure from the US several years prior, only this time, someone was leaving us. I'm not sure why it's so different, but goodbyes are harder for the ones who stay behind. This was only the beginning of us being the "stayers." More people were about to exit our lives.

Auntie Cora and her children saw us off at the airport. We stood hugging and chatting, drawing out the time before we had to go. I knew the drill. The one where we pretend we have more to say or something else that needs to be done. But really, we're just buying time, stretching out the minutes before the goodbye. Auntie Cora would land in the US about a twenty-five-hour drive from either of our families. Of course, we were hopeful we'd see each other again. But we were accustomed to goodbyes like this. Even if we saw each other again, it wouldn't be the same. She wouldn't be right down the road. Cora would no longer be a source of support for our family. Nor would she be right there to pray with me and give me a hug on bad days. That was the first goodbye.

Uncle David
After our time in the US, we returned overseas. Our good friend, David, who had visited us multiple times, was living at our house while we were gone. Though he had been to our area of the world many times for short-term trips, this was his first long-term stay. He was in our city for a full year. Like Auntie Cora, we met him as a family of two. He watched us grow into a family of four. Our kids wrestled with him, teased him, and went on adventures with him. He, too, became like family. When we landed back in our host country in January, we knew Uncle David

would soon be on his way out. In March, he would pack up and head back to the States.

We decided that someone as special as Uncle David deserved a fabulous farewell. This was the children's second big TCK goodbye. After reading about all the transitions and grief TCKs go through, we determined a nice trip would be a fun way to celebrate our friendship with Uncle David and say goodbye well. We'd make new memories to laugh about, and adventures would pop up along the way. And most of all, we could freeze time for a few days and pretend we weren't at the end of Uncle David's stay.

January 2020 came with it whispers of a weird sickness spreading. In February, the whispers turned into loud rumors. Ron and I decided on a destination in our state, in case the rumors turned out to be true and travel was hindered. We planned the trip for the second week of March. Uncle David would go out with a bang on an adventurous trip. We'd love him well and show him how appreciative we were for his partnership.

By the beginning of March, the rumors proved to be true and threatening and, our trip was canceled. We were positive we'd find a way to celebrate Uncle David well, but each day, the world became more chaotic. Warnings grew louder and louder. Talks of lockdowns. Concerns about hospitals collapsing in our country. Then it happened. Our country announced a full lockdown. It would begin in two days' time. Uncle David worried he'd end up stuck in our country long term, so he decided to fly back to the US the very next day. Out of all the ways we imagined saying goodbye, this was not it. From a distance, we talked with Uncle David in the parking lot of our apartment building. It was a swift goodbye. There was no time for one more meal together. No opportunity to show him how thankful we were for how he invested in our ministry and family. No time for lingering. Just a couple of cards our kids made to say thank you and a five-minute parking lot encounter.

We climbed the stairs to our apartment, our kids confused and concerned about what had happened. Why did we say goodbye so quickly? Why couldn't we share one more meal together? According to the research I had done on helping TCKs transition and grieve well, this was a giant flop. There was no last memory to record in our minds. There was no goodbye hug. No final words of encouragement. The relationship just was until it wasn't.

As COVID-19 made its flight around the world, spreading from one country to the next, our expat utopia melted like ice on a hot summer day. We were a large expat family before COVID—there were maybe ten American families in our city focused on mission work of some sort. By the end of 2022, only two families remained. Each goodbye was like Uncle David's. A quick, unexpected exit with much uncertainty as to whether the family would return. And no opportunity to absorb that last delayed conversation for the sake of being together just a bit longer. Nope. Each parting was swift, unexpected, and impersonal.

In the back of my mind, I wondered how these goodbyes would impact my kids. Of course, COVID-19 created many other concerns, like the collapse of the healthcare system in our state, loss of access to flights, and fears of sickness here, there, and everywhere. But these goodbyes—would the kids stop trying to make friends? Would they tire of trying when a goodbye seemed imminent in their expat lives? Would they have mental health issues when they were older because of the constant change and stress? Would they blame us for a childhood that kept them in a spin cycle of making and losing friends?

And then another question—could I reason that staying was worth all this? I trusted God to take care of me. He's my place of refuge. But my children were not yet believers. Would this life make them hate God? Or could they see the beauty in our family's freefall? The beauty of a life that reflects the great Shema: giving our whole being fully to our King. Would they someday understand that my heart's desire to please God leaves me no choice but to entrust their outcome to Him?

I'm a woman of intention. When I see a problem, I find a solution. The limbo of a problem with no solution unsettles my stomach. Our friends were flying away one by one, like brown leaves on a tired tree in fall. I reasoned the only way we could stay in this place was if I could find a solution to this problem. I couldn't stop the circumstances that were causing my children grief, but I could lessen the blows. I found a solution. We rested hard.

We were intentional about family time. Wednesdays have always been our full-stop day of the week. Phones off. Work off. Laundry and house cleaning are also off. It's a sabbath rhythm that keeps us fresh and ready for ministry. For one day, we fully devote ourselves to soul care, self-care, and family care. I would partially attribute our eight-year tenure to this habit.

Then COVID-19 came. Family days were different in lockdown. Now was the time we needed them more than ever, but how do you have a family day when your home is no longer a relaxing place? I will say, we have two savvy kids. They figured out quickly during those early lockdown days that mom and dad would do whatever we could to keep their spirits up. We used toy containers with wheels on the bottom and stacks of Duplos to play human bowling. We baked cakes and threw birthday parties for every stuffed animal in the house. We played boys versus girls "prank wars." Whatever we could do to laugh and connect was at the top of our to-do list.

We rested well as a family by intentionally planning activities that boosted our spirits. Although we couldn't take away the pain of goodbyes without closure and the lockdown, we could be an anchor for our kids' hearts. We could teach them that even when God calls you to a hard place, He will give you rest and allow you to find joy. I can't guarantee my children won't grow up and hate the work we've committed our lives to. But I can reduce the potential of that happening by spending time with my children so they know they will *always* be the priority over my ministry.

Jessica

As we neared the end of 2021, our souls were tired. Goodbyes had been numerous. Lockdowns were prevalent. And the world was a different place. But we had hope. Light was indeed at the end of this horribly long tunnel. The COVID-19 frenzy was slowing. Travel was opening, and ministry was restarting.

Then came the year of the atomic bomb. For almost six years, we had partnered with a local couple on our business. They knew our intentions for living in this place. They supported our work by helping us create and run a business that would give us access to our people. The wife became my best friend. I led her to the Lord. She was one of the locals who knew us and really got it.

Then, in the strangest turn of events, they announced they wanted out of the business. It was not profitable and had become a waste of their time, they reasoned. We were grateful for their partnership and understood their desire for financial gain. However, we did not understand their method of departure. They demanded a large sum of money and stopped communicating with us three days after their declaration. That was December 23. Merry Christmas, everyone. Within days, lawyers were involved because we discovered impropriety. My most trusted friend had deceived me. She now refused to talk with me other than to call for Ron, generally with a yell and expletives sprinkled in. What on earth was going on?

Jessica had become like a sister during the six years we worked together. She encouraged me when I lacked confidence. She was honest and pointed out my errors when I messed up. She helped me navigate hard parenting days. We were so close. I had trusted her with sensitive information. How could this happen to us? If I couldn't trust her as a friend, I was positive I could trust no one. The fear I had for my kids—that they would shut people out to avoid potential grief—was now threatening me. My walls started going up.

For five months, we lived in fear of being found out. Would they tell the authorities what we were doing? They had information that could land us in jail. That was a reason to flee for sure. Should we leave the country tomorrow with whatever we could take? Would they follow through on their threats to shut down the business without our permission? That would land us with no visa in just three short months. Life was so unstable. Within a week, they had knocked our entire lives off balance. We didn't know where we would live or what we would do when the dust settled. It was as if we were walking on two tectonic plates that could part without notice and swallow us up. We spent our nights in tears. Anger. Fear. Sadness. Grief. We spent our days strategizing. How do we answer their most recent demand? Would our lawyers implore us to sue? Could we stay? Did we want to run this business alone? Sleep eluded us.

For five months, every time we went to a grocery store or a restaurant, I worried we would run into Jessica. My heart was constantly on edge. But I also hoped we would run into them. I yearned for reconciliation. I begged God for it. If I had done something to warrant that dramatic departure, I wanted to understand and apologize for what I did wrong. But her walls were up, and reconciliation was not an option.

For five months, I dealt with an unsettled stomach while we were in the middle of a problem that remained unsolved. We were on unstable ground. I was sure I'd end up with a stomach ulcer. Our family in the States noticed the fatigue. We had survived two years of COVID-19 lockdowns, only to slide exhaustedly into a dramatic foreign business buyout. They saw the energy evaporating from our souls.

My dad had warned us when we left for the mission field nine years prior, "If you come back and God hasn't called you back, you won't have a room at my house." I knew his heart. It wasn't that he literally wouldn't take us in. It was his way of saying, "Veronica, I know ministry. This is going to be hard. It's going to push you to your limits. You'll want to flee. Stay. Stay where God has called you until He moves you to a new place. Stay in His will." That same dad, with a look of concern on his face during a video call in the middle of this nightmare, commented, "Honey, is it time to move on?"

Move on? This is not how I imagined our "move on" to go. I thought someday we'd move on celebrating what God had done in this place—leaving with a sense of accomplishment and joy. But this? Move on now? At this point, our exit would not be joyful or worth celebrating. It would be a departure of defeat. My dad had good reason to be concerned. He could see the mental and emotional toll the degrading phone calls and impending lawsuit had taken on us. But was this how God wanted to move us to a new place? We spent hours praying and seeking God's will as we walked forward.

Five months after Jessica's announcement, we finalized buying out the business. After much prayer and counseling from our supervisors, we felt compelled to stay. Yes, stay even in the middle of this terrible tailspin. God had not yet told us it was time to go. We were, again, resolved to stay and not flee from this foreign, now excruciatingly painful, place.

As we ended the buyout and began our journey as solo business owners, the storms did not relent. The following month, our last colleagues who had weathered COVID-19 alongside us announced they were moving back to the States. It was a quick departure. Within a couple of weeks, Anna's best friend left. Still reeling from the unexpected loss of my best friend, I had to pull myself together enough to sit compassionately in that hard place with Anna. It was as if we were in *The Hunger Games*. One by one, each of the other players got knocked out. Each elimination added more grief and pain to our hearts. Now it was just us. There were no colleagues who could come over late at night to pray with us when life fell apart. No one we could celebrate holidays with. Our kids' TCK friends were all gone. We were alone.

The following month, someone stole our credit card number, leaving us with no backup for purchases. Every vehicle our company owned in the city approached registration renewal. Being the only personnel in the state meant Ron was out of the house, spending large amounts of money in a few weeks to keep all the cars up to date. We were also responsible for paying three home payments and multiple national partners' pay. We were paying so many bills, our home office could barely reimburse us in time to pay the next thing. We spent the month alone, watching our money hop in and out of our account (but mainly out). Buying groceries was near impossible. How did we get here?

Finally, something good was on the horizon—our annual meeting with colleagues in our area. Our company scheduled it that year specifically to give rest to our families post-COVID. The free resort stay would include golf, water park days, meals, and amazing volunteers to watch our kids as we processed the last few years of ministry. As the meeting neared, we anxiously waited for our visa. Each day, we called the visa agent to see if it would be the day we could retrieve our passports and confirm our participation in this much-needed getaway. The days came and went, but our visa did not come. We missed the trip.

We were alone. Stuck on an island. Exhausted. And without enough money to buy normal groceries. Why,

TO STAY OR FLEE

God? What is the purpose of staying in this place if our bones become so brittle they break? Why walk us through such a long season of grief and anguish? It was no longer a question of if we would stay, but how it would even be possible. We didn't know that we could. Lord, we don't feel you leading us elsewhere, but how, God? *How do we stay in this place now?* Do you see us, Lord? We've been betrayed. We're alone. Stuck. Teach us. How do we stay?

"Come to me, all of you who are weary and burdened, and I will give you rest."[6] That was God's answer. Let Me give you rest. For two people who teeter on the edge of being workaholics, it was a full-time job to switch our brains to rest mode. But we saw it in Scripture and finally took the command seriously. Jesus often snuck away to a quiet place to rest and pray. If Jesus Himself felt the need to get away and rest, then I would be prideful to think I didn't need to do the same.

Rest came in a few different ways. First, we found soul rest. We took time with the Lord as much as possible to sit and tell Him our concerns. During this time, when it would have been easy to slide away from God, we made it our aim to pursue Him. One of the sweetest times of soul rest was a trip with our local church. Right after the last of our colleagues announced their departure, our pastor

---

[6] Matthew 11:28 CSB

invited us on a trip around the state and offered for our family to stay with his. His kids were the same ages as ours. Our whole family was grieving, but this healed our souls. Having a spiritual leader in our life care for us like that was one of the main ways the Lord comforted us.

We also rested emotionally by talking through our situation with a counselor and trusted colleagues. We were fatigued from months of emotional pain. We needed help to sort through it and come out healthy. The Lord gave our counselor and colleagues words of wisdom and encouragement. It was another way the Lord brought healing.

Finally, we chased after mental rest as if our lives depended on it. We desperately needed to turn off our phones and brains. One of our Christmas gifts to ourselves and the kids was a golf membership at a local resort that included pool access. Ron made a habit of going to the golf course to put his brain on silent and let the kids ride along with him on the cart. Our kids learned to swim again. I sat next to the pool, being still. Our brains disengaged from stress and engaged with one another. This was a recovery year post-COVID, so the resort offered a three-night stay at the hotel for the price of one. Prior to our financial constraints, we purchased so many of those packages we became preferred members of that hotel chain. I never imagined being able to afford a hotel like that, let alone be a preferred member. But I remember Ron saying to me when we were dealing with the buyout, "Veronica, this is the most taxing thing we've ever walked through. We could save up our money and stay one night at this five-star resort every couple of weeks. Don't you think our mental health is worth it?" As frivolous as that sounds, it was one of the healthiest things we did. Our phone signal was lacking in that area, which meant our bodies and brains could truly relax. We may have spent part of our children's college fund on those hotel stays, but it was worth it to rest as a family. The Lord continued to bring healing.

Grieving a Separation

Grieving a separation is weirdly difficult. When an individual dies, it's final (at least until heaven). Friends and family are compassionate and sympathetic. But grief that results from separation is often overlooked. People move all the time, we reason. "It's part of life." We try to convince ourselves that changes in our support system are a common occurrence. So, there isn't as much compassion or support for the person who's been left behind by a close family member or friend. People assume the grieving person can hold on to the hope of seeing their friend again. But, in many ways, that makes it harder. The person left behind knows their friend is still alive and kicking on this planet, but their lives are no longer in sync.

This weird grief is heartbreaking, but it holds onto an annoying hope for reunion which may or may not happen. If a reunion happens, it will probably be only for a few short days. Then the tornado of grief and pain starts swirling again when friends go their separate ways. Grief for a person who was once *the* person but is now somewhere drifting away in another place is complicated. It's for a best friend. An aunt. Grandma. A person who is still loved but is no longer present.

What have we learned about recovering from painful times of grief? Make rest a priority. Act like your life depends on it. It's not being lazy; it's intentionally creating space to process. Sit with the Lord for soul care. Talk with others for emotional care. Play hard for mental care. If Jesus Himself needed rest, we need it even more.

The Spitting Cobra in My House

When Spiritual Warfare Gets Real

Wise Advice

When we first prepared to leave for the mission field, seasoned missionaries shared stories of the spiritual warfare they'd faced. Honestly, it was terrifying to listen to these tales of missionary affliction. One person gave an account of an evil spirit squeezing them until they could hardly breathe. But during our initial training, one man put all my apprehension into perspective. What he shared about spiritual warfare has shaped the way I face hard times overseas. His main point was that in the midst of spiritual warfare, God is present. He knows what's happening and has allowed the hardship. But God is sovereign and always victorious. These truths from Scripture are the spoiler alert to the Story that trumps them all.

At the end of two years in lockdown and a disastrous business buyout, we needed rest. Instead, the enemy hit us with a week of the most heated spiritual warfare we'd ever faced.

Because I don't want to share this story and spark fear, here's the spoiler alert: God allows intense battles, but He is always sovereign and always victorious. He prepares us beforehand. He's with us in battle. We don't win battles by our strength, but in our weakness by His strength. Victory in spiritual warfare is His alone.

Childhood Snake Experience

There aren't many things I dislike about where we live, but I hate the snakes.

Growing up, we had the sweetest (and dumbest) golden retriever. Jakey and I were best friends. He did his best to bring abundant joy to my life. In his golden retriever way, this meant making me pet him, snuggling close, and bringing me gifts. His gifts were generally still alive. He brought me birds, baby bunnies, a skunk, and even turtles as he aged. But my least favorite gift from Jakey was a mouthful of snakes.

I remember the day I called him in from the pasture like it was yesterday. He ran toward me with black rope-like objects dangling from his mouth. As he got closer, I noticed the ropes were moving. Then it clicked. He had a mouthful of snakes. Three of them, still alive, wiggled and squirmed while suspended from his mouth. He must have found a snake nest. I screamed and ran. He thought I was excited and wanted to play tag. There I was, screaming and sprinting through the yard like a crazy person, chased by a dog who looked like the offspring of Medusa. Finally, our other malamute dog noticed my plight. He pulled the snakes from Jakey's mouth, grabbed them one by one, and violently shook them until they died.

Because of this childhood experience, I had a very firm warning for Ron when we moved overseas: the day I see a poisonous snake in our yard is the day I move. Period. Ron knows I rarely change my mind. Some would say I'm stubborn. I say I'm committed. At any rate, Ron knew I was serious. It would take an act of God to change my heart.

B-Day

A few months after our business buyout and sending off the last of our colleagues, we found a baby spitting cobra in our house. Our house that is a full story off the ground on pillars. Ron and I had just sat down on the couch, ready to relax and enjoy an hour of calm after putting the kids to bed. Suddenly, our dog, who was lying on the rug, bobbed his head up and down curiously. We turned on the light and saw it—a baby snake. It was only six inches long, but where there's a baby, there must be a mommy, I thought. Ron reached out to grab it. The snake, yet to be identified as a spitting cobra, rose its head to challenge Ron's hand.

I screamed like a baby, now standing frozen on top of the couch. I'm not sure why standing on the couch made me feel better. This baby snake, or its mother prior to birth, had already climbed twelve feet off the ground and slithered into our house. It could easily ascend the eighteen inches that separated me from the floor.

Ron's endeavor to rescue our family from this baby snake was an intense one. He had to keep me calm while staying laser-focused on killing the snake. He hushed me, reminding me that my screams might bring the kids downstairs. We did *not* want them to know about this. They might never sleep again. Then he ordered me to come down from my eighteen-inch perch and get a shoe so he could kill it. "Nooooo! I can't get down!" I challenged. He quickly responded, "Do you want this snake to be loose in our house, or do you want to walk over to the closet to get a shoe?" I swiftly conceded. With a quick wham, the snake died a shoe-induced death.

I slept the entire night attached to Ron, jump-waking every time the sheet hit me weirdly. Our noble canine kept guard at the foot of the bed. I feel he deserves a space on our family photo wall in a hero's cape. That baby cobra could have hung out inside our house, growing into a full-size cobra, if it wasn't for Thor.

The day after this baby cobra sighting, we had an overnight staff retreat at a local hotel. We packed quickly in the morning, lights fully on, watching every step. I insisted Thro stay right by my side. Ron, without my knowledge, had messaged a wildlife expert. Mr. National Geographic confidently told Ron the only snake matching the picture I took was a spitting cobra. I lived in ignorant bliss about this for twenty-four hours. Then, during our staff retreat, I found out one of the hotel staff was a wildlife expert. I made the senseless decision to show him the picture of our intruder. In my mind, this little greyish-black snake was likely the Asian version of a garter snake. It would relieve stress to hear it wasn't dangerous.

The wildlife expert relieved no stress. He told me the same thing Mr. National Geographic told Ron. That little baby snake in our house was a spitting cobra. If it had bitten anyone, it would have likely released all its poison in one go. My husband, who reached out his hand two inches from the little guy, could have died if it had bitten him. Sometimes I wish I asked fewer questions.

After the staff retreat, we stayed at a friend's house. Ron took a day or two to check our home and plug any holes to ensure we had no mommy or sibling snakes free-loading at our house. He meticulously scoured the place, pulling each piece of furniture away from the wall, looking in each nook and cranny. He even stuck his head into our dark attic to ensure we didn't have a family of cobras up there. After the first day, Ron wasn't comfortable with us returning. He said the cat rubbing up on him almost gave him a heart attack. And if Ron about had a heart attack, as low drama as he is, I'd already be in the cemetery.

But a baby cobra breaking into our elevated home wasn't even the worst of the warfare that week. Three days after B-Day (that's Baby Cobra Day) was a Sunday morning. I woke up really sick. I had been sick for a few days with a stomach bug. Moving from place to place made it easy to become dehydrated. I went to the hospital to see if I needed treatment of some sort. They confirmed I needed IV fluids.

The emergency room night doctor must have been tired, because prior to receiving my blood test results, he decided I needed 875 different medicines and didn't explain a single one. Then a nurse proceeded to give me medicine for my stomach pain and nausea. I pressed, "Wait—I don't have any stomach pain or nausea. Why am I getting medicine for it?" She replied, "Never mind. The doctor ordered this medicine, so you take it." I should have protested, but I didn't. She jabbed the medicine in the IV, and that's when things went haywire.

My body had a severe reaction to the medicine. I was pretty sure yelling at her ninety-five times to get a doctor and some Benadryl was going to be the last thing I did. Those poor nurses didn't even know what the brand-name American drug was.

For nearly ten minutes, my heart skipped almost every other beat. The heart rate monitor screamed its own warning, beeping frantically as my heart rate ran 154 beats per minute while I was sitting completely still. When the doctor finally arrived, he defended his decision rather than fix my very obvious problem. He argued my symptoms warranted the medicine, even as the chaos of the heart rate monitor shrieked at him in the background. "Just get me some Benadryl!" I demanded.

The scariest part of all was that I went blind. Well, not fully blind, but I could only make out shapes in the room. There I was—blind, on the verge of heart failure, and by myself in the ER. And the only people who could help me were the ones who had accidentally almost killed me.

I attempted to message Ron during the ordeal. Thankfully, my habit of swipe texting had created decent motor memory. I typed something like, "Get your butt to the hospital. They are killing me!" But I wasn't sure what I *actually* sent because I couldn't see it. Nor could I see his response. Did I really want the nurse, who had almost killed me, to read my husband's reply to "Help, the hospital is murdering me!"

Meanwhile, Ron was talking to the fire department about our spitting cobra situation. When we told friends about it, they thoroughly freaked us out by responding, "Well, that baby's mom must be somewhere. Hopefully, it's not in your house." The only actionable advice we received was to talk to the fire department.

It seemed a bit dramatic to bring them into it. What were we supposed to say? "Hi, we had a six-inch baby cobra in our house a couple of days ago. It's dead now, but we know nothing about cobras. Could you come over and check under our beds for us? We're scared to go to sleep tonight."

As over-the-top as it felt, we reasoned following our local friends' advice was probably the responsible thing to do. After all, we didn't want our kids to get cobra poison spit at them while putting together a puzzle on the living room floor—the stinking living room floor. Well, the fire department not only sent a snake expert, they sent a snake expert plus fourteen other firemen, blazing through our subdivision in two trucks with lights on and sirens blaring.

Two of the firemen wore full-face helmets like astronauts. Were they on their scooters, ready to grab lunch, when they were called to an emergency snake situation? Maybe they thought there was a big cobra currently in our house. This would've provided another story to share at family gatherings to wow their in-laws. I feel kind of bad. Our little escapade was probably a disappointment.

Anyway, as all fifteen firemen came blazing up to our house in two firetrucks, my husband received my text about being murdered at the hospital. Our two kids were with him. They were exhausted and fussy from sleeping in four different beds over four nights. The kids were also jumpy because they knew there was a snake *around* our house; they just didn't know it was *inside* our house.

Ron quickly called in response to my message. He needed to decipher if this was loopy Veronica exaggerating about a bad hospital visit or truly on-her-death-bed Veronica.

"Are you okay? What happened?"

I relayed my story, the heart rate machine still blaring in the background at the hospital while the fire truck sirens blasted in the background at our house. Two competing alarms pronounced simultaneous emergencies in our lives.

Ron replied, "Uh, do you really need me to come right now? I mean, that sounds so scary. But also, I'm at the front gate. Two fire trucks are pulling into our house right now. How bad are you almost dying?"

We made a split-second decision for him to carry on with his reptile adventure. He'd call a friend and ask her to join me immediately, if possible, at the hospital. The doctor eventually relented and shot a dose of hydrocortisone in my IV. Within fifteen minutes, my heart rate was back to normal, but my heart was not. What a fear-inducing moment! Our home was no longer a sanctuary. The hospital staff made a mistake that almost cost me my life. Where could we find shelter and safety? Ron and I had both danced with death that week. Terror filled my heart.

By the time Ron made it to the hospital, I was on the edge of the bed, ready to pull out the IV line. I had no interest in putting my life in the hands of these doctors and nurses any longer than necessary. But medical experts in the US disagreed. Over a phone call, they informed me I should keep an IV in my arm for the next twenty-four hours in case the hydrocortisone wore off and the allergic reaction returned.

I wasn't about to stay at that hospital alone, so we arranged for our kids to spend the night with friends from church. Then, Ron and I enjoyed a wonderful overnight date in a hospital room on the fifth floor. He brought games from home and some yummy food to help ease my heart. We knew wallowing in fear and apprehension wouldn't help us. But our hearts were weary from all the warfare that week. It was hard to be genuinely joyful. There was an elephant in the room. We were under attack.

The next day, I was direct with the hospital's HR department about my unpleasant stay. Despite everything, I tried to be polite. The hospital sent a gift basket with a card to my room as an apology. This is the letter I think they should have attached:

Dear Veronica,

We're sorry we tried to kill you while your husband was at home with the fire department, searching your house for a family of spitting cobras. We won't try to kill you again, we promise.

Love,
The Hospital

Battle Plan

I hope that time remains the most dramatic week of our life overseas. Following that experience, fear hounded me, but I reminded myself of Scripture's spoiler alert. God is sovereign, and God will be victorious. In this, I can find peace.

None of these events caught God off guard. He is sovereign. Just like in the story of Job, God allowed us to go through it. Like Job, my response needed to be to stand firm and worship. "The Lord gives, and the Lord takes away. Blessed be the name of the Lord" (Job 1:21 CSB). God will put me in a battle that's impossible to win on my own so He can fight for me. The nations will notice, just like the people around Job noticed. This battle was an opportunity to learn and deepen our faith.

It was also an opportunity for those around us to see the staying power of God. He knew what we would face in these post-pandemic years. He had sprinkled just enough help along the way to get us through. Our pastor and local church rallied around us. Colleagues went out of their way to care for us. I'm confident the Holy Spirit had a part in prompting these people to support us through the storm. God knew this was coming. He could stop it at any moment. When I remember God is aware of my situation and in control, facing hard things is less intimidating. When I focus on my Father, the work of the enemy isn't so scary. Like when Peter walked on water, when I focus on Jesus, I have the courage and confidence to walk through a storm. But when the wind is where I fix my gaze, I begin to sink.

God is also victorious. In 2 Chronicles 20, King Jehoshaphat received word that multiple armies had joined to declare war on him. They were coming. What was his response? Initially, fear. But then he resolved to seek the Lord. He proclaimed a fast and gathered the people to pray. "We do not know what to do, but we look to you" (2 Chronicles 20:12 CSB). As the people of Judah sought the Lord, He answered them through a prophet. They were to march toward the other armies, but they wouldn't have to fight. Standing still, they would see the Lord's salvation.

As they traveled toward the battlefront the next morning, Jehoshaphat implored the people to believe in the Lord their God. He appointed singers to walk ahead of their army, praising God. What a battle plan! Just sing the other army to death. But the Bible tells us, "At the very moment they began to sing and give praise, the Lord caused the armies of Ammon, Moab, and Mount Seir to start fighting among themselves" (2 Chronicles 20:22 NLT). In the end, Jehoshaphat's enemies died, and the nations around Judah noticed the strength of their God. Our God is victorious. Do I believe that when I face spiritual warfare? Or do I think I have to be strong enough, brave enough, and bold enough to face the situation alone? I must hold tight to the truth that my God will win in the end.

God is Victorious

The spoiler alert to every believer's story is God's sovereignty over warfare and victory over heartache. Sometimes we don't see the victory here on earth, but it will happen. Through that year of trauma and heartache, God gifted us with multiple opportunities to see His power over the evil around us. Pictures of heaven—that's what He gave us.

One stressful evening, Abe made several poor choices. Normally, I respond to the kids with patience. But because I had the heavy weight of our business disaster on my mind, his behavior ticked me off. I freaked out on him. He was wrong, but I was more wrong because of how I reacted. I was the adult, after all. A few hours after my snap reaction, the Lord convicted me. I humbly approached Abe and asked for forgiveness. We reconciled.

The next night, Abe called me into his bedroom. He told me he wanted to follow Jesus. This was not the first time. It had been a frequent occurrence for several months. When we pressed him previously on why he wanted to follow Jesus or what it meant, he couldn't articulate it. But this time, he insisted and could explain perfectly, "Mom, I really want to follow Jesus. I don't want to wait any longer!" Ron and I asked why, and I'll never forget Abe's response. "Because last night I sinned against God when I broke those new pencils. When you got so mad at me, I realized I was wrong and needed Jesus's forgiveness." God is sovereign. God is victorious. What the enemy meant for evil, God meant for good.

Several months after B-Day, a vision God had given us for our work here was finally fulfilled after seven years of service. When we opened a local business, we felt firmly that the business wasn't just for us, but for others who sought to do mission work. For years, we worked toward the fulfillment of this vision. We trained local believers, hired them as staff, and welcomed them into our family. But no one stayed long-term. They were afraid.

But after the buyout was complete, everything changed. We started a program with two other families. Together, we train local believers to reach out to the unreached people in our state. At the end of each training period, some of these people come on as staff in our business. Recently, two new staff led six people to the Lord in two weeks. God is sovereign. God is victorious. What the enemy meant for evil, God meant for good.

Finally, on a three-day family camping trip, Anna announced one evening that she was ready to follow Jesus. What was her "why"? She didn't want to be alone through hard or scary times. When I heard her answer, scenes from the prior year flashed through my mind—moments when stress and trauma nearly defeated and left me in tears. Times when people around me had pained me deeply to the point I couldn't hide it from my children. Each time she saw me cry (which was more than I care to admit), she asked me what was wrong. Friends shared our concern that seeing so much pain could upset Anna. Each time she saw me cry, I did my best to give her a kid-appropriate explanation. I wanted to be truthful, but also reasonable about how much I shared. Then I emphasized through the tears that without Jesus, I'd be a disaster—unable to walk through this hardship. God is sovereign. God is victorious. What the enemy meant for evil, God meant for good.

About the Author

Missionary Veronica Stone has served in three countries over the last ten years. During her time overseas, she has led volunteer groups from America, mentored new missionaries, and started a successful platform business that allows local missionaries to be sent out. Formally educated as a teacher, she passionately invests in those around her. To her kids, she's a quirky homeschool mom who mixes movement into learning time. To the staff at her platform business, she is the relentless trailblazer who insists there is always a way! And to the local partners that she mentors, she is a listening ear ready to encourage.

Reviews

Thank you for reading *How to Stay and Not Flee*. I hope you enjoyed it. Please take a few minutes to leave a helpful review on Amazon and Goodreads. I appreciate your time and support!

Love,
Veronica